FRONTIER FORTS
and *Outposts* of
NEW MEXICO

FRONTIER FORTS
= and *Outposts* of =
NEW MEXICO

Donna Blake Birchell

Published by The History Press
Charleston, SC
www.historypress.com

Copyright © 2019 by Donna Blake Birchell

All rights reserved

Cover images courtesy of the Open Parks Network and the author.

First published 2019

Manufactured in the United States

ISBN 9781467140782

Library of Congress Control Number: 2019948157

Notice: The information in this book is true and complete to the best of our knowledge. It is offered without guarantee on the part of the author or The History Press. The author and The History Press disclaim all liability in connection with the use of this book.

All rights reserved. No part of this book may be reproduced or transmitted in any form whatsoever without prior written permission from the publisher except in the case of brief quotations embodied in critical articles and reviews.

This book is dedicated to my father, William Blake, whose love of history and the military sparked a fire in me. You are so missed.

This book is also dedicated to all of those who have served and continue to serve New Mexico and the United States in all branches of the armed forces. It is with a grateful and humble heart that I thank you for your service and our freedom.

Lastly, I would like to dedicate this book to all of those, on both sides, who suffered greatly under the blanket of progression and misunderstanding.

CONTENTS

Acknowledgements	9
Introduction	13

PART ONE: LONGEST INHABITED NEW MEXICO FORTS

Fort Bayard (1860–Present)	27
Fort Craig (1854–1885)	36
Fort Cummings (1846–1873)	49
Fort Marcy (1846–1868)	54
Fort Selden (1865–1890)	60
Fort Stanton (1855–Present)	74
Fort Sumner (1862–Present)	85
Fort Union (1851–1891)	104
Fort Wingate (1862–1925)	120

PART TWO: NEW MEXICO FORTS INHABITED FOR OVER FOUR YEARS

Fort Bascom (1863–1870)	129
Fort Burgwin (1852–1860)	130
Fort Fillmore (1851–1862)	132
Fort McLane (1860–1864)	133
Fort McRae (1863–1876)	134
Fort Thorn (1853–1859)	136

Contents

PART THREE: NEW MEXICO OUTPOSTS AND CAMPS
Fort Butler (1860)	139
Camp Cody (1916–1919)	139
Camp Ojo Caliente (1859–1882)	140
Fort Barclay (1851–1854)	141
Fort Conrad (1851–1854)	141
Fort Dawson (1851–1852)	142
Fort Defiance (1851–1861)	142
Fort Lowell (1866–1869)	144
Fort Tularosa (1872–1874)	144
Fort Webster (1852–1853)	145
Fort West (1863–1864)	146
Bibliography	147
Index	153
About the Author	160

ACKNOWLEDGEMENTS

First and foremost, I would like to thank Samantha Villa, whose faith in me helped me to believe in myself. Thank you, my friend.

I would also like to thank my wonderful family: Jerry, Michael, Sherrie, Justin and Amanda, who are the lights of my life! Also, to Missy and Robert Garriott, thank you for listening to me drone on about the forts and history. Much love to you all! Your love and support mean everything to me, and without you, I would be nothing.

Thank you, also, to Richard Estes for his *stunningly brilliant* subject suggestion! I truly appreciate the input!

I want to give a huge thanks to Carol Estes, my dear friend, who accompanied me on a great journey to Fort Craig and Fort Union and provided great navigation as well as the best travel company ever! Thank you for your continued friendship and support. I love you!

To Sheila Martinez, my awesome friend, thank you for sharing the story of your great-uncle Private First Class Samuel Smith, Navajo Code Talker, with me. It is an honor to relay his story.

To my outstanding editor, Lindsey Givens, who was always there with gentle guidance and a genuine interest in the subject matter of this book, you have been invaluable. Thank you so much for your awesome support while keeping me on track!

Finally, I would also like to thank you, the reader. Without your support, this journey would be meaningless. Your encouragement to continue is uplifting and inspiring, and it is the thing that pushed me through some tough times.

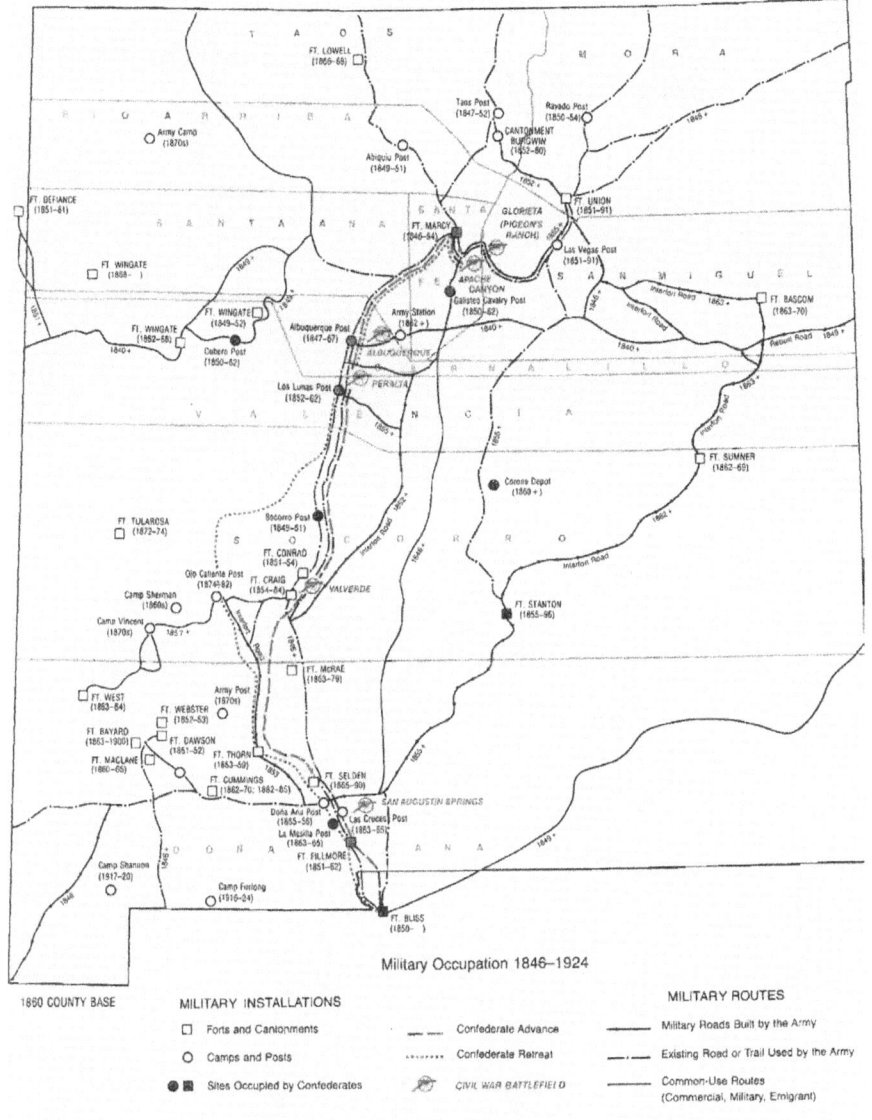

Map of military installations in the New Mexico Territory from 1846 to 1924. The territory was well protected along El Camino Real. *Courtesy of the author's collection.*

INTRODUCTION

New Mexico Territory

Desolation and loneliness ruled the New Mexico Territory during the days of the Old West; it was inhabited primarily by the Native peoples and the Spaniards until the arrival of the Anglo-Americans around 1846. The territory provided shelter, clothing, food and water for all the people who settled there and was highly cherished by each culture. The Anglo-Americans saw great opportunities in the region and wanted to seize them, while the Natives sought to preserve their heritage lands; thus, the conflict began.

War is not politically correct, so it is extremely difficult to write about the conflicts that occurred between the Anglo-American and Native cultures without stepping on any toes, but both sides of the coin will be shown with as much historical accuracy as possible. Atrocities occurred on both sides and spread distrust and eventually hate, but this book's intention is not to pass judgment or rewrite history. Alternatively, this book aims to tell the history of each of the forts and their purposes as accurately as possible.

The forts and outposts of the West were first established to protect travelers along the Santa Fe Trail and the Goodnight-Loving Cattle Trail from attacks by the Natives who roamed and claimed the area. As the attacks escalated, the United States government sought to eliminate the threat, and the main duty of the forts became to eradicate the tribes that were deemed the most troublesome in the eyes of the government—namely, several of the Apache (*N'de*), Navajo (*Diné*) and Comanche tribes.

Introduction

The New Mexico Territory was full of harsh realities as the area struggled to become a state. The people who lived there not only had to deal with outlaws but also suffered continued attacks from the Native people who were not happy about the arrival of Europeans, Spaniards or Anglos. New Mexico had a long and arduous road between its beginnings as a Spanish colony and its achievement of statehood in 1912. The cards had to fall just right for the United States government to accept New Mexico as a candidate for statehood. Because of the long-lasting Mexican occupation of the New Mexico Territory, the United States was leery to accept it into the Union, thinking that the region might still be loyal to the Mexican government. This, however, turned out to be false, and the territory was reluctantly instated into the Union. The beautiful land we know as New Mexico became the forty-seventh state and was known by many monikers, including the Sunshine State (thirty years before Florida adopted the name), the Colorful State, the Cactus State, the Spanish State, the Land of Opportunity, the Land of the Delight Makers and the Outer Space State; however, New Mexico is most widely known today by its current nickname, the Land of Enchantment, which was first adopted in 1906.

Manifest Destiny, 1845

The concept of Manifest Destiny is widely defined as "the belief, or doctrine, held in the middle or latter part of the nineteenth century, that it was the destiny of the United States to expand its territory over the whole of North America and to expand and enhance its political, social, and economic influences."

This doctrine made the United States feel it had the right to confiscate any and all lands it chose in order to perpetuate the progress of the nation. This confiscation was done without any regard to who may have already held claims to the land, which, as one can image, did not sit well with Native tribes who did not recognize the United States as their government. This doctrine led to the many uprisings and attacks by Native tribes that took place for over forty years during the Great Western Expansion.

Introduction

Treaty of Guadalupe Hidalgo, 1848

The signing of the Treaty of Guadalupe Hidalgo in Mesilla, New Mexico (in the courtyard of the modern-day Double Eagle Restaurant), in 1848 officially ended the war between Mexico and the United States. The treaty states, according to Article I of the document: "There shall be firm and universal peace between the United States of America and the Mexican Republic, and between their respective countries, territories, cities, towns, and people, without exception of places or persons."

The treaty also states that the property rights held under Mexican law would be respected by the United States. The Spanish land tenure system was a foreign concept to the American idea of private land ownership. In the Spanish system, land grants were used to divvy up land in the New Mexico Territory—using arroyos, mesas and sometimes even trees as boundary markers. One of the largest land grants was the Maxwell Land Grant, which encompassed 1,714,765 acres of land in Colfax County and reached as far as Las Animas County in Colorado. An interesting note of Lucien Maxwell, owner of the Maxwell Land Grant, is he was the largest landowner in the New Mexico Territory and is buried in a lonely cemetery in Fort Sumner, just a few yards from Billy the Kid. There is a large marble headstone that commemorates Maxwell's life and accomplishments, but the cemetery is barren, rocky and hardly the place where you would imagine placing a man of his wealth for his final rest.

Civil War in New Mexico

When most people think of the Civil War, they think of the immense, often brutal, struggles between the Northern and Southern states that sometimes pitted brother against brother, neighbor against neighbor, and father against son east of the Mississippi River, but few thoughts go to the battles in the West. During the war, Confederate forces invaded New Mexico from Texas and Mexico and took control of the capital, Santa Fe. Their ultimate plans included seizing the New Mexico and Arizona Territories and their silver mines in order to fund their campaign, and they did this while making their way to the Colorado gold fields. Without an intervention from the brave soldiers in the northern forts, this plan may have become a reality.

Introduction

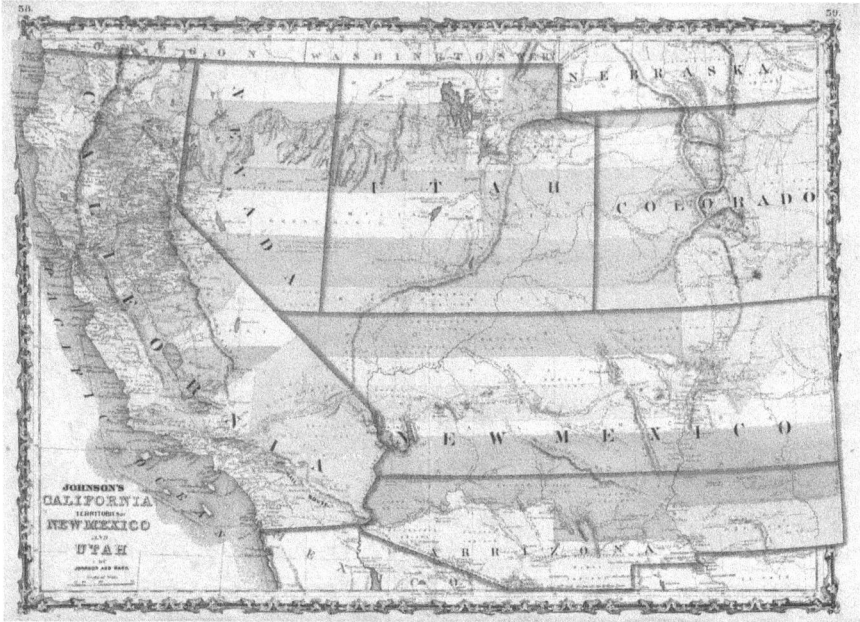

Until 1850, the New Mexico Territory extended well into what is now Arizona. At that time, Arizona included the southern half of New Mexico. *Courtesy of the Library of Congress.*

Scrimmages and full-fledged battles occurred on New Mexico soil in places like Albuquerque and Valverde, and the battle in Glorieta Pass became known as the "Gettysburg of the West." More complete descriptions of these battles will be given in the Fort Craig and Fort Union chapters.

During the Civil War, the casualties were so devastating that men of fighting age became scarce, prompting a new wave of soldiers to enlist. These recruits unfortunately included young children, who were turned away at first but later utilized as drummer and errand boys. For this reason, the Civil War was often referred to as the "Boys' War." Many of the fighting children had been rendered orphans due to the war and medical epidemics that swept the land, and they felt that the conditions in the army were better than the conditions in the orphanages and foster homes.

The Confederacy became a true threat to New Mexico on July 23, 1861, when Colonel John R. Baylor of Texas marched into Mesilla, New Mexico, and claimed all lands south of the thirty-fourth parallel for the Confederacy. Tough choices had to be made by soldiers who had sympathies toward the South; many defected, including Henry H. Sibley, who was a major at this time and would go on to play a key role in the Confederate invasion of New Mexico.

Introduction

APACHE RAIDERS

Who were the Apache raiders and why did they cause the region so much turmoil? Names such as Geronimo, Mangas Coloradas, Nana and Victorio come to mind when thinking of their fierce leaders, who fought the insurgence of the Anglo and Spanish settlers, miners and traders who were determined to make this part of the country their own—without concern for the people who already occupied the region.

Intolerance, ignorance and mistrust played huge roles in the struggles that ensued from prejudice felt on both sides. The Natives, who had called this land their home for centuries, were being invaded by a relentless group of people who were certain the land they traveled on was already theirs. Each side did not understand the competing ways of either culture, so turmoil ensued.

The United States government, in its plan to bring the Natives to their knees, employed many Natives as scouts, a practice used by the United States since the Revolutionary War. Of course, these men were viewed as traitors by their own people, as they were used to try to outsmart the tribes with their own tactics. These scouts were housed at nearly every

Indian scouts were used to track and translate for the United States Army and were paid with U.S. dollars, which they had little use for. *Courtesy of the Library of Congress.*

INTRODUCTION

Chief Geronimo was one of the fiercest leaders of the Apache. His name means "one who yawns." *Courtesy of the Library of Congress.*

frontier fort in the territory, especially Fort Wingate, and were thought of by the government, at first, as employees rather than soldiers. Although the scouts worked for the government, they retained their own style of tracking and war tactics, never giving over to the white man's ways of war.

Once the Civil War ended in 1865, the Natives were enlisted into the army as official soldiers and paid the same wages as the others. Their service in the United States Army would continue until 1914.

Introduction

Military Life

Life in the military is not easy, as it is often portrayed on television or in the movies, especially in the forts of New Mexico. It took a great deal of determination for the soldiers to perform, often in harsh conditions and while wearing heavy woolen uniforms, all the orders given to them from their commanding officers. Many books and memoirs of soldiers recount the terrible abuse inflicted on the enlisted soldiers by some of their commanders, which incited many to desert. Due to the forts' isolation, the soldiers' separation from their families and female companionship combined with the fact that the average age of the men was seventeen, alcoholism also became a huge problem at the forts. Refusing a drink of whiskey was considered a personal insult and oftentimes resulted in a fracas within the ranks. Although most deployments lasted only two years in the New Mexico Territory, this time seemed endless to those who served.

Supplies at the forts were scarce and, many times, unusable. Military forts and outposts in the far reach of the territories would often have to rely on their own devices in order to survive. Hunger was rampant among the soldiers, and they were sometimes forced to kill and eat their own horses in order to live. Soldiers were often forced to trade their brass buttons, pieces of random wire and pins for food, since army pay was often nonexistent for many months and sometimes years.

Small towns popped up close to the military installations and provided not only a break from fort life but also female companionship, whiskey and much-needed provisions. These towns, which were mostly farming communities,

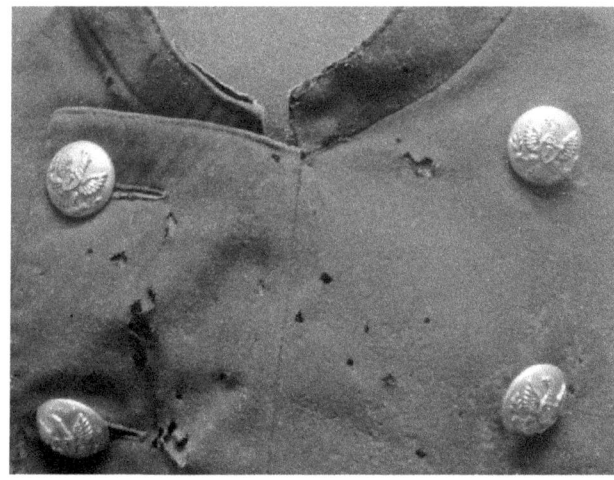

Soldiers would use the brass buttons from their uniforms to barter for food and other rations when they were low on supplies. *Courtesy of the Library of Congress.*

INTRODUCTION

got far more than they bargained for on many occasions, as we will see in the story of Loma Parda, a town near Fort Union. Gambling was a huge problem for the military in New Mexico; when soldiers left their posts to enjoy festivities in town, many often returned penniless. A law was enacted that stated, "Any business owner caught with people under 21 years of age, or an enlisted man, in a gambling establishment, [is] subject to a $100 fine and losing his license."

Buffalo Soldiers

The 9th and 10th Cavalry Regiments and 125th Infantry of the United States Army were best known as the Buffalo Soldiers. Known to be fierce fighters and great warriors, they were considered the elite of the units in New Mexico and served well at several of the state's forts and outposts.

Credit for the Buffalo Soldiers' name is given to the Cheyenne tribe by the Buffalo Soldier National Monument. It is said that after the Cheyenne faced the Tenth Cavalry in battle, they were not only impressed by their fighting skills but also intrigued by their physical appearance. The African American soldiers, with their mahogany skin tone and tightly curled hair, resembled the American bison in the eyes of the Natives, so they gave them the name "Buffalo Soldiers." Others say it was the Kiowa who were first to give the moniker; this fact is debated among historians. The name stuck, and several thousand of the 175,000 African American troops who served in the Civil War were stationed in the New Mexico Territory between 1866 and 1900. The African American soldiers of the Tenth Cavalry felt so honored by the name that they incorporated a buffalo symbol into their regimental crest.

According to War Department records, the segregated African American troops were consolidated into units, which were then pared down to two infantry regiments and two cavalry units. The Buffalo Soldiers first arrived in the New Mexico Territory at Fort Sumner in 1866, when the members of the 57th and 125th Infantry Regiments camped there while en route to Fort Stanton and Fort Selden. These units soon joined the men of the famed 9th Cavalry, who were deployed at Forts Craig, Bayard, Cummings, McRae, Selden, Stanton, Tularosa and Wingate. It was from these various forts that the 9th Cavalry would join in the efforts to eliminate the Apache war chief Victorio. After their service

Introduction

Left: Buffalo Soldiers earned respect in the U.S. military through their reputation of being fierce and brave fighters in the many wars they fought. *Courtesy of the Library of Congress.*

Right: Members of the Twenty-Fifth Infantry, Buffalo Soldiers, saw military action from the American Indian Wars to World War II. *Courtesy of the Library of Congress.*

in the Indian Wars, as well as the Lincoln County and the Colfax County Wars, the 9th Cavalry left the territory in 1881. No Buffalo Soldier troops would serve in the region again until 1887, when the 10th Cavalry was stationed in Fort Bayard.

These brave soldiers not only provided protection for the settlers, travelers and mail carriers along the Rio Grande corridor but also helped build most of the forts in which they were stationed. The New Mexico Territory was not a favored place to be stationed, and the forts there had a high desertion rate. This meant that the troops who decided to fulfill their obligations there, including the Buffalo Soldiers, were brave, strong and, many times, fearless—all the qualities it took to live in the New Mexico Territory.

Buffalo Soldiers served at Fort Bayard from 1888 to 1896 as the Twenty-fourth Infantry, at Fort Selden from 1888 to 1891 and at Fort Stanton for three months in 1896. The Twenty-fifth Infantry Regiment and the Ninth Cavalry Regiment were the final Buffalo Soldiers to serve in the New Mexico Territory at Forts Bayard and Wingate between 1898 and 1899.

Introduction

The Ninth Cavalry went on to serve during the Spanish-American War and were thought to be the actual first Americans to top San Juan Hill, despite this honor being given to President Theodore Roosevelt's Rough Riders in most history books. No matter the correct order in historical data, it was New Mexico soldiers who first planted the guidons on top of San Juan Hill.

California Column

The California Column consisted of ten Union companies of the First California Infantry, five companies of the First Regiment California Volunteer Cavalry, the Second Regiment California Volunteer Cavalry and Company B and the Light Battery A of the Third U.S. Artillery, who, in 1862, marched over nine hundred miles in four months from California, through the Arizona and New Mexico Territories, to the Rio Grande, near modern-day El Paso, Texas. They advanced from California to stop the invasion of a small Confederate Texan force led by resigned Union soldier Henry H. Sibley; this force was also known as Sibley's Brigade. The campaign was launched in April 1862 from Yuma, Arizona, where the heat was already beginning to soar in the Mojave Desert and the poor soldiers were issued standard wool uniforms for their journey. Word was eventually sent to Colonel Edward Richard Sprigg Canby, commander of the Union forces in the New Mexico Territory, that the column was indeed on their way and would be able to help with the troubles he was having near Albuquerque and Santa Fe.

Colonel James Henry Carleton, who would later prove to be a rather ruthless man, sent small groups of men ahead of the main line to secure supplies along the then-dismantled Butterfield Overland Mail Route. The stations along this route still had food and grain, which was stored for the purpose of providing troops with supplies. Confederate forces were able to intercept these attempts of advancement and engaged the column forces in two small skirmishes in the Arizona Territory.

Along their journey to New Mexico, Carleton and his men also encountered the great Apache chief Cochise, who was hiding out from the United States government in Apache Pass with five hundred of his supporters. At this time, it was thought that Cochise could have been responsible for the deaths of over five thousand settlers and Mexican travelers during his eleven-year reign of terror in the region. The Battle

Introduction

Left: General Edward R.S. Canby was a career army officer and Union general. He faced Confederate general Henry Sibley at the battles of Valverde and Glorieta. *Courtesy of the Library of Congress.*

Right: General James Carleton was well known for his hatred of the Native American culture and spent his career proving that fact. *Courtesy of the Library of Congress.*

of Apache Pass was the first time Cochise had engaged in warfare with the United States government. The battle was won by the Union forces, thanks to the introduction of the mighty howitzer, which the Union soldiers were able to use to their advantage from the ridge of the pass. Cochise and his army retreated and would not be captured until 1872.

After this battle, Carleton and his soldiers were able to reach the New Mexico Territory without further trouble. By the time the California Column arrived at the Rio Grande, the Confederates had already begun their retreat to Texas. The column followed Sibley's Brigade to Franklin, Texas, where they quickly captured the town and advanced farther, to Fort Quitman. The column spent the rest of their service in West Texas, where they prevented invasions of the New Mexico Territory by Confederate forces.

Introduction

After the Civil War

It is amazing to think that there are still Civil War–era forts still in operation today. Fort Stanton and Fort Bayard have been in existence since the beginning of the Civil War, and you will read about their amazing histories in this tome.

Many of the larger forts that will be mentioned are now National Monuments and National Historic Landmarks whose histories are protected by the federal government so that they may be enjoyed by generations to come. These facilities are manned by amazing volunteers who have dedicated their lives to the preservation of history, and they should truly be commended for their valiant efforts!

Preservation of the Past

As the passage of time threatens to erase the evidence of the past, efforts are being launched to protect the structures and ruins that still exist of the frontier forts in this book. In the words of the director of the New Mexico Historic Sites, Patrick Moore: "If we do not preserve them, we really lose sight of who we are as a people; it's a complex relationship that we're constantly grappling with."

Preservation is the key to sustaining our heritage and history. Many of the sites mentioned in this book are under siege by a new enemy—the elements. Since most of the forts were constructed with the resources available in their remote locations—mud and clay for adobe bricks—every rain shower, flood and windstorm threaten to take away another layer of history. Unfortunately, this has already occurred at many of the earlier forts, which were not inhabited for long lengths of time, leaving only a few bricks or a foundation footprint as evidence of their existence. Forts such as Union and Selden are enacting heavy preservation efforts in order to save their fragile legacies. The once majestic adobe and brick structures have been reduced, in many cases, to rounded-off shadows of their former glory. Tarps, raw lumber and resurfacing materials (mud) are being utilized to support the crumbling walls. Through the monumental efforts of park personnel, volunteers and the public, these efforts will not be in vain.

You can assist in these efforts by visiting these awe-inspiring sites, paying the nominal (if any) entrance fees, spending a few dollars in the gift shop

Introduction

Preservation efforts at most of the forts have reached a critical level. Without help, many of the forts will soon disappear. *Courtesy of the author's collection.*

Introduction

and donating what you can for the preservation efforts. We must work hard to keep this history alive for future generations to enjoy. Our history is fading fast.

During the course of this book, you will notice that many of the players in these histories are the same throughout. This is because most of the same military units were used to build and protect each of the frontier forts that spanned the territory. Whether the units were loyal to the Union or Confederacy, they all played an integral role in not only the amazing history of New Mexico but also the history of the United States as a whole. We owe a great deal to these men and women, who were thrust into an inhabitable environment to battle fierce opponents with spirits as great as their own.

Part One
LONGEST INHABITED NEW MEXICO FORTS

Fort Bayard (1860–Present)

The border between southwestern New Mexico and Texas has always been a volatile region, plagued by outlaws who preyed on gold and silver miners, several Apache tribes, and in later years, the famous Mexican revolutionary Pancho Villa.

Silver City, located a mere eight miles from the border, has a colorful history with some of the most notorious characters in New Mexico history, including Billy the Kid, Madame Millie, "Dangerous Dan" Tucker, Butch Cassidy and the Wild Bunch—Ben Lilly, Geronimo, Victorio, Cochise, Kit Carson and Poker Alice. Fort Bayard, named for General George Dashiell Bayard who died in 1862 during the Battle of Fredericksburg and who also served in New Mexico and Arizona prior to the Civil War, also calls Silver City home. The fort is described by locals as "eerily beautiful," as the quiet remains of a once-vibrant fort still stand at attention along the stone walkways. One-, two- and three-story buildings, which once served as the quarters, mess halls and hospitals of the fort, are still intact and ready for inspection.

The fort, established in 1860 by General James Carleton of the California Column to protect miners of the Pinos Altos Mining District at the base of the Santa Rita Mountains, as well as the growing numbers of cattle drivers that were traversing the New Mexico Territory to reach Kansas, saw its

Robert Parker (*far right*), better known as Butch Cassidy and members of the Hole in the Wall Gang were known to wander the Silver City region. *Courtesy of the Library of Congress.*

share of action in its location in the southwestern part of New Mexico, near the Gila National Forest, and was chosen for its springs and views of the Apache War trails that surrounded the mining camps. After just one year of existence, the young Fort Bayard would suffer its first attack from the Apaches during the Apache Wars, which lasted from 1861 to 1886.

Seven soldiers from Fort Bayard were awarded the Congressional Medal of Honor between 1877 and 1882 for their actions during battles against the Warm Springs and Chiricahua Apaches. Corporal Clinton Greaves, one of the Buffalo Soldiers and a Medal of Honor recipient, was awarded the medal in 1877 for the acts of heroism he performed in the Florida Mountains near Fort Bayard. He and his fellow troops were able to negotiate the surrender of a band of Apaches but soon found they were surrounded. Greaves, through hand-to-hand combat and excellent shooting, was able to allow his troops to escape. The second recipient,

Training horses to perform well during battle was vital to saving the lives of Fort Bayard soldiers, and drills were frequently enacted to test these skills. *Courtesy of the Library of Congress.*

Sergeant Thomas Boyne, was awarded the medal in 1879 for his bravery in action against the Apaches in the Mimbres Mountains. Also in 1879, Second Lieutenant Mathias Day of the Ninth Cavalry (Buffalo Soldier) was awarded the medal after helping a fellow soldier to safety under heavy fire in Las Animas Canyon, and Sergeant John Denny and Second Lieutenant Robert T. Emmet were awarded medals for the same action. The final recipients were Sergeant Alonzo Bowman, who was awarded one for his bravery at Cibicu Creek, Arizona, in 1881, and Sergeant John Schnitzer, who was awarded a medal for his bravery at Horseshoe Canyon, New Mexico, in 1882.

To ignite the settlers' hatred of the Apaches even more, Apache warriors began killing prominent citizens of Silver City and Lordsburg. The founder of Silver City, New Mexico, John Bullard, was killed in 1871 by Cochise, creating a massive manhunt. In March 1883, the Apaches, led by Chato, killed well-known judge Hamilton McComas and his wife, Juniata, and kidnapped their six-year-old son, Charley, in Thompson's Canyon in the Burro Mountains while the family was traveling between Silver City and Lordsburg. The couple was found stripped naked and splayed out on the ground, the buckboard was broken apart and one of the horses was also dead. Chato would later say if the judge had kept quiet and not let out a whoop and whipped his horses when he saw the war party, the pursuit by the tribesmen would not have occurred. The judge had sent word to their oldest son, David, who worked at a silver mine in Pyramid City, near the modern-day ghost town of Shakespeare, that they were coming for a visit, but he had no way of warning his family of the high rate of Apache activity in the area. When news of the judge's and his wife's horrific deaths reached David, he was unable to accept it and died two years later.

Even though a company of soldiers from Fort Bayard had set out immediately after learning about the ambush, the Apaches broke off into three factions and were almost impossible to trace as they fled to Mexico. Everyone feared that Charley was lost forever, since it was the tradition of the Apaches to kill captives that cried or were too much trouble. Many years later, it was reported that the numerous Apache raids of Cananea, Mexico, were led by a white man. Speculation arose that this man could possibly have been Charley McComas, who was never found. Although it was never proven, the rumor persisted for several years.

Another interesting story related to Fort Bayard involved Sergeant James Cooney, a scout for the Eighth Cavalry Regiment. During one of his many scouting missions, Cooney came upon a large deposit of gold and silver, eight miles up a creek that is now called Mineral Creek, in the Mogollon Mountains north of the fort. The soldier kept his find a secret until 1876, when he returned to the location with two friends to work his claim. While riding to Alma, New Mexico, Cooney and his two friends Jack Chick and Mr. Buhlman were ambushed and killed by Victorio's Warm Springs Apache band while they were on their way to warn settlers in the area of an attack at Cooney's mine on April 29, 1880. The sergeant's brother, Michael, and several miners from Birchville, later called Pinos Altos, drilled, blasted and chipped a sepulcher for the remains of Sergeant Cooney out of a large boulder, where he is still interred today. As the years passed, a small cemetery formed around the boulder tomb, although some of the headstones were washed away by a flood. The tomb, known as Cooney's Tomb, is now a roadside attraction. Michael Cooney spent the rest of his life looking for gold in the Mogollon Mountains, and the canyon in which his body was found four months after an apparent Indian attack is called Cooney Canyon in the Gila Wilderness.

LONGEST INHABITED NEW MEXICO FORTS

Buffalo Soldiers

The 38th U.S. Infantry replaced the original 125th Infantry that was stationed at Fort Cummings in the beginning of the Civil War in the New Mexico Territory. In the ranks of the 38th was an unusual soldier by the name of William Cathay, whose true name was Cathay Williams. Williams is the only woman who is known to have been a part of the all-black regiment.

Born into slavery in Independence, Missouri, Cathay Williams wanted her freedom more than anything in the world, and she was willing to risk it all to obtain it. After the Civil War broke out, Cathay was freed by Union troops and went to work for the Federal army as a paid servant. During her servitude, she worked for Colonel Thomas Benton and General Philip Sheridan as a cook and laundress. While traveling with the military, Cathay saw some of the worst battles of the Civil War firsthand. Once the Civil War ended, Williams did not want to return to poverty, since she had enjoyed the financial gains she earned during employment, so, in November 1866, she enlisted as Private William Cathay in the Thirty-eighth Infantry—also known as the Buffalo Soldiers.

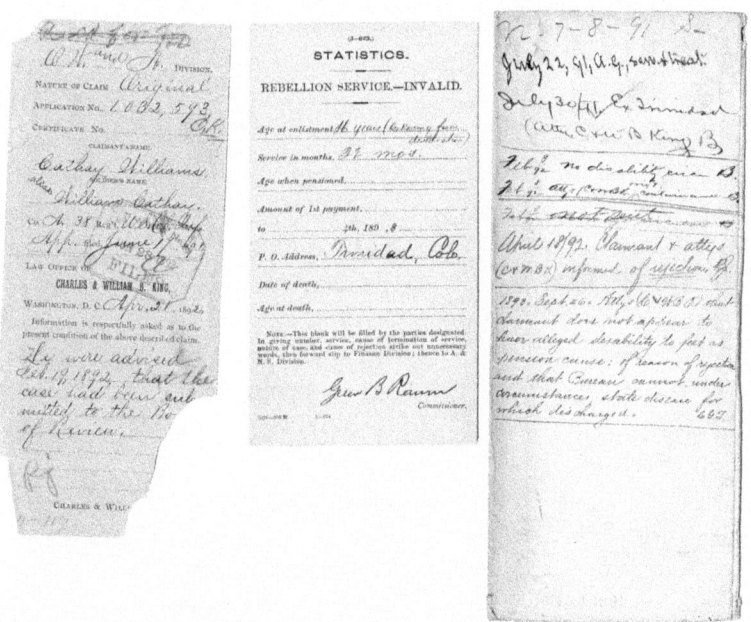

Cathay Williams's disability rejection papers. These came after she was revealed to be acting as a man. Note that the alias on the papers is William Cathay. *Courtesy of the Library of Congress.*

A statue honoring one of the nineteen Buffalo Soldier Congressional Medal of Honor recipients, Corporal Clinton Greaves, graces the center of Fort Selden's grounds. *Courtesy of the Library of Congress.*

Within a four-month period, she and the other soldiers marched from Missouri to Kansas and finally to Fort Union in New Mexico, which was five hundred miles away. In September 1867, the company marched to Fort Cummings, where they would remain until June 1868. (A typical infantry soldier during that time period carried a large amount of equipment, which included a cotton hack sack for food, a canteen, a rifle or musket, a bedroll, a cartridge box, a knife and a sidearm and had to carry this equipment in any weather while wearing a woolen jacket and pants and heavy boots.) Although Cathay was strong, it became increasingly difficult for her to carry the pack, mainly due to her diminishing health.

Cathay began to grow tired of the infantry lifestyle and longed to leave the army. When she arrived at Fort Bayard on June 6, 1868, after marching from Fort Cummings, Cathay grew ill and was hospitalized on July 13 for neuralgia (a neurological disorder, which was, at the time, a bogus diagnosis, since she could have had several ailments). During her examination by the fort surgeon, it was discovered that she was a woman. On October 14, 1868, William Cathay was given a certificate of disability and honorably discharged with a statement that said "he" was of "feeble mind and body" and "unable to do military duty." Williams stated that once the men of her regiment learned she was a woman, they began to treat her poorly, so she returned to Fort Union to work as a civilian cook for a resident colonel. From there, Cathay traveled to Pueblo, Colorado to work as a laundress before moving permanently to Trinidad, Colorado.

Due to her failing health, Williams filed for a pension from the United States Army with the claims she was suffering from deafness, rheumatism and neuralgia—all acquired during her time in the army. Her application was denied because her discharge certificate indicated that she was in a feeble condition before her enlistment and that her service in the military was not legal. Cathay Williams's fate after this rejection is unknown, since she is not listed on any census reports after 1900.

Another notable Buffalo Soldier was Private Walter Loving of the Twenty-Fourth Infantry Band, who served at Fort Bayard and was said to be able to play any instrument and sing any song. He was sent to the Philippines during World War II, where he learned the language and sang it to music. When the Japanese heard of his talents, they arrested him and accused him of being a spy and using his music as code. Unfortunately, his great talents would lead to his beheading by the Japanese near the end of World War II.

John J. Pershing, who would later be known as "Black Jack" Pershing, began his illustrious military career at Fort Bayard as a second lieutenant with Troop L of the Sixth Cavalry on September 30, 1886, after his West Point graduation. During his time at the fort, Pershing participated in several campaigns against the Apaches and would receive citations for bravery for his actions. Pershing's job at Fort Bayard was to establish a heliograph system—a signaling mirror, or wireless solar telegraph, system that helped soldiers communicate between Fort Bayard and Fort Stanton by pivoting mirrors and using the flashes as letters. Invented by a British engineer, the heliograph was developed by the United States Army Signal Corps to develop better military communication and the telegraph system. By 1886, there were twenty-three heliograph stations utilized in Arizona and New Mexico, each one twenty-five miles apart.

After he successfully established a heliograph system at Fort Bayer, Pershing was transferred to Fort Stanton, New Mexico, to assist in the campaigns against the Mescalero Apaches there as well. During his free time, Pershing and his friends Lieutenant Julius A. Penn and Lieutenant Richard B. Paddock would enjoy hunting and attending Hispanic *bailes* (dances). The three were nicknamed "The Three Green Ps."

After the Indian Wars

With the surrender of the last Apache leader, Geronimo, the need for frontier forts declined and many were scuttled; the four-hundred-acre Fort Bayard was deactivated with its last garrison in 1900 for this reason. Due to its great location, Fort Bayard soldiers enjoyed some of the best health of any troops stationed in New Mexico. This fact was noted by army surgeon general George M. Stemberg, who suggested the fort hospital remain open and available to the growing numbers of tuberculosis patients in the United States. In 1899, the five fifty-man barracks of the fort were authorized as tuberculosis sanatoriums by the War Department and stayed that way until 1922. Fort Bayard quickly became known as the army's first sanatorium.

In 1899, seven contract nurses arrived at the fort, along with two dieticians—one being registered nurse Dita H. Kenny, who would become superintendent of the United States Army Nurse Corps in 1901—to treat tuberculosis patients. When patients came to Fort Bayard, they were generally underweight and sickly in appearance. A plan was developed to supplement their regular diets with a concoction of two raw eggs, two tablespoons of cod liver oil and salt and pepper with lemon. Strangely enough, this diet began to work after just two months. The practice of using paper spit cups and plates, which were incinerated each day, also worked to stop the spread of the disease, and this plan was implemented by Major Daniel M. Appel, an army surgeon. The average lifespan of a person born in 1900 was only forty-five years, and one in seven people died of tuberculosis, which was often referred to as the "white plague." Under the direction of a tuberculosis victim in 1903, Major Private Dr. George Bushnell, a leading tubercular physician at the Fort Bayard Hospital, became the leader in the research and development of treatments for this devastating disease. Dr. Bushnell would often play music in the hospital in the belief that it lifted the mood and soul, leading to quicker healing.

By 1922, the fort was given to the Veterans Administration, which turned the facility into a Veterans Administration 145,000-square-foot hospital that could house 1,250 patients. The victims of mustard and chlorine gas attacks in World War I were sent to Fort Bayard because of New Mexico's climate. A method of utilizing mirrors to reflect the sun onto their lungs for treatment was popular but ineffective. The old fort was destroyed in the expansion, leaving the cemetery as the only ghost of the its past. Fort Bayard Memorial Cemetery is part of the National Cemetery system and has been on the National Register of Historic Places since 2002. The first

Fort Bayard's layout was exceptional. It was long thought to be one of the best-looking forts on the frontier. *Courtesy of the Library of Congress.*

person to be interred at the Fort Bayard National Cemetery was Sergeant David H. Boyd of the Third U.S. Cavalry on October 10, 1866. The Fort Bayard National Cemetery also participates in the Wreaths Across America program, which places fresh evergreen wreaths on the graves of United States veterans at Christmastime.

New housing and hospitals surrounded the parade grounds along Officer's Row. World War II saw Fort Bayard reactivated as a military installation to hold a group of German Prisoners of War from 1943 to 1945—just like many of the other forts and towns in New Mexico. A Solarium for tuberculosis patients, a movie theater, duplexes for medical offices, nurse's quarters and seven doctors' and officers' quarters were built on the site between 1902 and 1910.

The state of New Mexico eventually took over the site and used it as a state hospital and long-term nursing facility. The state still runs a hospital at the fort, although many of the buildings have fallen into disrepair.

Fort Bayard Today

Still vital today, Fort Bayard is in use as a National Historic Landmark and hospital for the state of New Mexico. Tours by the Fort Bayard Historical Preservation Society are available on request on Saturdays at 9:30 a.m. The Preservation Society also mans the museum from 9:15 a.m. to 1:00 p.m.

Recently, members of AmeriCorps have been assisting in the restoration and preservation efforts at the fort's impressive Officer's Row. The fort has also partnered with the local Apache tribe to produce the popular Native American Film Series.

Each September, Fort Bayard celebrates the rich history of the fort by hosting Fort Bayard Days, which features a parade, period dressing, reenactments and a military ball.

Directions and Information

When traveling from Silver City, New Mexico, take Highway 180 east to Santa Clara. This trip will take you approximately ten miles for twenty minutes. Turn left onto Fort Bayard Road, which will lead you to the Fort Bayard National Historic Landmark.

If you are traveling from Deming, New Mexico, take Highway 180 north to Santa Clara. (Do not be fooled by the town of Bayard, which is east of Santa Clara on County Road 356). Turn right onto Fort Bayard Road, and take another right into the fort site. This trip will be forty-five miles and approximately fifty-five minutes.

Fort Bayard National Historic Landmark
40 Fort Bayard Road
Santa Clara, New Mexico 88026

Visitor Center contact information:
To book a tour, please call these numbers.
(575) 388-4477
(575) 574-8779

FORT CRAIG (1854–1885)

When you travel along Interstate 25, south of Socorro, New Mexico, you are actually retracing a famous route used by Spanish colonists, Mexican settlers and Native tribes for hundreds of years: El Camino Real de Tierra Adentro, which translates to "the Royal Road to the Interior." As the Spaniards, under the leadership of Don Juan de Oñate, made their *entrada*, or journey, into what is now known as New Mexico in 1598, they traveled along the Rio Grande, which served as a great water and food source for them. The villages and settlements along the El Camino Real are some of the oldest in North America, as the trail was used until the late 1800s before the railroad system rendered it obsolete.

Oñate was sent by the king of Spain to explore and conquer new lands for the crown, so as he, and the hundreds of soldiers and settlers who followed him, journeyed down the 1,500-mile-long trail, they made it a Royal Highway for Spain. El Camino Real would continue to be the oldest and

Don Juan de Oñate was an early Spanish explorer who settled the Santa Fe region of New Mexico. He was known for his cruelty to the Native people. *Courtesy of the author's collection.*

longest-used road in Mexico and the New World until it was replaced by the arrival of the railroad in 1885.

In 1849, a garrison was sent to Socorro, New Mexico, by General Stephen Kearny to help protect the El Camino Real region. The Socorro Garrison was replaced by Fort Conrad in 1851, and in 1854, it was renamed Fort Craig, after United States Army captain Louis S. Craig, who served in the Mexican-American War. He was garrisoned with troops from Fort Conrad when, in 1852, he was murdered by some deserters he was following in California after he unsuccessfully tried to win them over with kindness. By 1861, Fort Craig was the largest fort in the Southwest with a troop strength of over two thousand men.

Fort Craig was located in a desolate area of the New Mexico Territory and shared concentrated regimental forces with Fort Union and Fort Marcy. These troops included Colonel Christopher "Kit" Carson and his New Mexico Volunteer Infantry Regiment. Carson lived in the Officer's Quarters and took great pleasure in sitting on a rocking chair on the porch while the cool evening breezes shifted through the fort and surrounding countryside. He found Fort Craig to be quite pleasant despite the complaints from his men.

Flanked by the Rio Grande to the east and surrounded by mesas and mountains, Fort Craig was situated perfectly for a vantage point on a flat plain. The men stationed there were able to see any possible attacks that may have been headed their direction.

One of the most striking landmarks at Fort Craig is the Black Mesa, which dominates the landscape to the north of the fort. The volcanic Mesa de la Contadera, which is sometimes referred to as El Contadera Senecú or Counter's Mesa, and is now called the Black Mesa, is where Confederate troops took a stronghold and observed the movements of the Union troops housed at Fort Craig during their attempted occupation of New Mexico.

Built in 1854, Fort Craig rose up from the desert floor to become one of the most important fortresses in the New Mexico Territory—or, as it was known at that time, the Department of New Mexico. Surrounded by mountains, the fort was at a slight disadvantage, but it was still one of the most important forts in the New Mexico Territory.

The Butterfield stage route started at Fort Craig, opposite Valverde, on the west side of the Rio Grande, then followed the river down to Paraje and on to Fort McRae (which now sits in the middle of Elephant Butte Lake). The route then traveled on to Engle and Fort Selden before it reached Massacre Mountain, Fort Cummings and Cooke's Peak. One of the soldiers' duties at these various forts was to protect the mail route from attacks perpetrated by Natives and outlaws.

As frontier forts go, Fort Craig was said to have been a good place to be stationed, but it had its faults, including leaky roofs, crumbling walls and crowded conditions. Although isolated and sometimes dangerous, the fort had many activities for the men, which included dances and dinners with the local ladies. Cultural items, such as books, magazines and newspapers, were available to keep the soldiers updated on the events happening back home.

A plethora of wildlife was observed around Fort Craig in soldiers' journals, including grizzly bears, black bears, deer, wolves, panthers (cougars), wildcats, weasels, pronghorns (antelope) and bison (buffalo). Soldiers also noted the presence of swans, pelicans, wild geese, ducks, cranes, blue herons, turkeys, quail, blackbirds, cardinals and snowbirds. All this wildlife gave the soldiers plenty of hunting opportunities.

Christopher "Kit" Carson, an Indian fighter and frontiersman, would take command at several forts in the New Mexico Territory, including Fort Craig. *Courtesy of the Library of Congress.*

Saloons and houses of ill repute were said to have also been available to the soldiers in nearby town of Socorro, New Mexico. The presence of fort and the soldiers that lived there caused an economic boom for these types of establishments in the region. Caches of buried whiskey bottles were found during archaeological digs in the area—not surprising, since alcoholism was common among soldiers.

Battle Strategy

In 1862, General Henry Hopkins Sibley led a rebel army of over 2,500 men up the Rio Grande to Fort Craig in the hopes of conquering the Union fort and continuing his campaign northward to Albuquerque and Santa Fe. Sibley's ultimate goal was to grasp the riches in New Mexico to fund the rest of his journey to Colorado, where he expected to find a treasure-trove of gold. Sibley was enthusiastic in his efforts, since he had just captured several small installations in the newly established Confederate Arizona Territory. In anticipation of Sibley's arrival, based on information given to him by Paddy Grayson's spy company, Union colonel Edward R.S. Canby began to move his troops from Santa Fe to Fort Craig as a show of force against the Confederate invasion.

Before officially arriving at Fort Craig, the Rebel forces worked nightly raids to probe Fort Craig's defenses; at one point, they were successful in driving off several hundred head of cattle. Supply trains, which were under heavy guard, were cut by Confederate maneuvers, leaving Fort Craig in almost a state of siege before Sibley's army arrived. As the soldiers of Fort Craig watched the formation of Confederate troops assemble near the Rio Grande and on the Black Mesa, it became clear that a full-out battle would not bode well for the Union. However, to the surprise of the Union troops, who did not know the Rebel's supplies were greatly limited, the Confederates kept their distance.

Another reason behind the Confederates' hold was an ingenious plan devised by Colonel Canby: he had soldiers place "Quaker Guns" on the dirt berms in and around the fort. These "cannons" were debarked logs placed on massive gravel bastions in formation in order to look like actual

Sitting silently on the earthen bastions, the Quaker cannons (fake guns) caused the Rebel forces to bypass Fort Craig, since they believed it was too heavily armed. *Courtesy of the author's collection.*

cannons from a distance. A soldier's hat was occasionally placed on them as well to give the appearance of the cannons being manned and ready for battle. In 2014, the Bureau of Land Management reconstructed portions of these earthworks in honor of the soldiers who original built and defended Fort Craig. This tactic was used during the Revolutionary War by Colonel William Washington, cousin to George Washington, the first president, against British forces in Connecticut, resulting in the surrender of 150 British troops.

The Rebel forces were unsuccessful in taunting the Union troops into battle, so they decided to give the fort a wide berth and start a stare-down, if you will, between the two armies. Sibley and his Confederate troops eventually decided to move north to cut off the fort's supply routes from Santa Fe; this movement would result in the Battle of Valverde.

Battle of Valverde

On February 21, 1861, the Battle of Valverde was fought; it was later touted as one of the bloodiest fights of the Civil War, although its story is rarely told. When the Civil War is discussed, it is generally only thought to have happened in the eastern, midwestern and southern states, such as Pennsylvania, Virginia, Tennessee and Indiana. However, there were several decisive battles that occurred in the New Mexico Territory, and the Battle of Valverde was one of them.

During the battle itself, Canby dispatched a group of cavalry, infantry and artillery forces under the command of Lieutenant Colonel Benjamin Roberts to a critical ford on the Rio Grande. It was there that Sibley was attempting to cross the river and cut off all communications from Santa Fe to Fort Craig. Roberts made the decision to send the cavalry and infantry ahead, since the artillery was slowing them all down.

Confederate Major Charles L. Pyron, with four companies from the Second Texas Mounted Rifles, had been sent ahead by Sibley to scout the ford for Union activity and to support Lieutenant Colonel William Scurry and his Fourth Texas Mounted Rifles. When they arrived, they were surprised to find Union troops already at the ford.

Pyron and Scurry joined forces, and the Union artillery moved into place. The Union forces did not charge the Confederate line, although the statistics were in their favor. The Union troops shot artillery rounds at the Rebel troops, who were not able to respond in kind due to the fact they were armed

Mesa de la Contadera, also known as Black Mesa, is a foreboding landmark near Fort Craig and was a Confederate camp site. *Courtesy of the author's collection.*

with only pistols and shotguns; this created a stand-off. In the meantime, Canby left Fort Craig with most of his forces to help at the ford, but he left a group of militias to guard the fort in his absence. Once he arrived at the scene, Canby left two infantry regiments on the west bank and crossed the remainder of the river. Union artillery continued to assault the Confederate soldiers, and the Union gained the upper hand.

Hearing of the Union movements, Sibley gave field command of his Fifth Texas Mounted Rifles and parts of the Seventh Texas Mounted Rifles to Colonel Tom Green. They were meant to reinforce the Confederate line while he remained in camp. The lancers from the Fifth Texas Mounted Rifles, under the orders of Green, advanced forward and were greeted with heavy fire from the First Colorado Volunteers, causing them to withdraw. After assessing the situation, Canby decided not to commence a frontal attack on Green but instead began to put pressure on the Confederates' left flank. This was accomplished by Colonel Kit Carson and his untested New Mexico Volunteers crossing the river and advancing on the Confederates, which also pushed Captain Alexander McRae's artillery battery.

Green ordered Major Henry Raguet to lead an attack on the Union's right flank, which bought the Texans enough time to assess the situation.

The Union forces repulsed Raguet's charge, but as they were being pushed back, Green ordered Scurry's men to attack the Union's center. Using three waves, Scurry's men were able to strike near McRae's artillery battery, take their guns and shatter the Union's line. Knowing they were defeated, Canby ordered a retreat and returned to Fort Craig.

This battle cost the lives of 111 Union soldiers; there were also 160 wounded and 204 captured or missing. Sibley lost upward of 230 men as well as most of his supplies; because of this, he decided not to attack Fort Craig. For many of the same reasons, Canby decided not to pursue the Confederates as they moved north.

This fierce battle lasted for only a day, but it was said to "involve the kind of tough, stand-up fighting" that was horrific beyond belief. Descriptions from the Texan Confederate soldiers stated, "They screamed like maddened cougars, made a savage charge armed with pistols, double-barreled shotguns and Bowie knives." The odds were in the Union's favor, as they had 3,800 men against the 2,500 Rebel troops, but the Confederate troops would triumph on this day. Reports accounted that they were jubilant at the win and said, "We made the Yankees dance to our music." After their defeat, the Union troops retreated to Fort Craig. Since this was the first battle of

The once beautiful Officer's Quarters at Fort Craig are a stark reminder of the harshness of the environment in which the fort existed. *Courtesy of the author's collection.*

Henry Hopkins Sibley joined the Confederates when the Civil War began and invented the Sibley Tent. He received five dollars for each tent sold. *Courtesy of the Library of Congress.*

the Civil War to be fought on New Mexico soil, many of the territory's forts were named for Union soldiers lost during this battle.

After the battle, Sibley turned his sights northward to Albuquerque and Santa Fe. It is said that he took these cities without a fight, although some accounts claim that there were cannonball volleys between the two armies in Albuquerque. After the citizens complained that the armies were putting them in danger, the lobbing of cannonballs ceased. While in Albuquerque, the Confederates camped in what is now the South Valley, on the property that now houses the Red Horse Vineyard Bed and Breakfast, but made their move northward to Santa Fe in their quest to claim the New Mexico Territory for the Confederate army.

Buffalo Soldiers

After the Civil War, members of the segregated Buffalo Soldiers would serve at Fort Craig. The infantry units served from 1866 to 1869, and the cavalry unit served sporadically from 1876 to 1881 to help with the Indian Wars and the pursuit of Native leaders.

According to the Fort Craig brochure, Union general William Tecumseh Sherman found the Buffalo Soldiers to be a remarkable group of soldiers, and he said, "They are good troops; they make first-rate soldiers, are faithful to their tasks and are as brave as the occasion calls for." This was high praise for a group of African American soldiers, who were oftentimes freshly freed slaves and whose loyalty was questioned by the army. The Buffalo Soldiers would repeatedly prove their critics wrong.

Indian Wars

After the Civil War, the Native tribes became the focus of the United States government, and the functions of the frontier forts returned to protection from the Indian raids. The Apache warriors and chiefs who were stirring up trouble in New Mexico were Geronimo, Mangas Coloradas, Nana and Victorio. Much of the soldiers' time at the forts was spent pursuing these men, who were unhappy with the deplorable living conditions on the reservations. The spread of disease and the lack of food and supplies prompted these men to rebel against the government of the United States.

When Victorio decided to escape the San Carlos Reservation and take his people back to their homeland, Fort Craig became a staging post for the United States Army. Victorio and most of his people—many of whom were women and children—were killed in Tres Castillos, Mexico. The remaining members of his band were captured by the Mexican Army. After Victorio's death, eighty-year-old Nana joined Geronimo and his band to fight the United States Army for four years, until their surrender in 1885. Nana died in captivity at the age of ninety-six, still defiant.

Once the Native threat to settlers on the frontier became nonexistent through the death and capture of their leaders and tribes, Fort Craig was abandoned in 1885. The fort was then auctioned off to the Valverde Land and Irrigation Company. The fort was eventually donated to the Archaeological Conservancy by the Oppenheimer family before it was transferred to the Bureau of Land Management (BLM) in 1981. Fort Craig is now a part of the Bureau of Land Management Special Management Areas and listed on the National Register of Historical Places.

Fort Craig Today

Manned by many knowledgeable volunteers, today, Fort Craig is a National Historic Site. After following Highway 1 to the historic site, drivers happen upon an isolated, quiet set of ruins in the middle of the New Mexico high desert, which provokes an almost reverent feeling. The adobe ruins are a stark reminder of the once bustling community of soldiers and civilians who lived along the Rio Grande.

It is hard to imagine today, but this was once the largest fort in the territory, with over two thousand men living in its walls. The only residents of the fort today are the occasional jackrabbits and collared lizards. The wind, which has sculpted the adobe ruins, swirls around visitors' heads, and if they listen closely, they can almost imagine the sound of horses' hooves pounding the soft, sandy soil as they do their maneuvers on the parade grounds. The Visitor's Center at the fort houses a small museum of diagrams and period photographs, as well as merchandise, which give you a true sense of the size of the fort in its heyday.

One of the darker moments at the fort happened recently; it was discovered that over twenty bodies had been looted from the Fort Craig Cemetery. This prompted the exhumation of 67 bodies by federal archaeologists to prevent further looting, although over 251 graves are in the cemetery. The exhumed bodies included 39 men, 2 women and 26 infants, who were moved to the Santa Fe National Cemetery. Apparently, grave robbing is a profitable business and had been taking place in the cemetery for many years. Archaeologist found evidence of the looting, including plastic bags and soda cans, left inside coffins. Many of the identities of the deceased will never be known because of the carelessness of these looters. On April 1, 1876, the United States Army removed 140 soldiers who were interred at Fort Craig during the Civil War, and sent them to the Santa Fe National Cemetery as well.

Recently, a macabre story surfaced of a local Vietnam veteran who had displayed the mummified remains of a Buffalo Soldier in uniform in his home for many decades. These remains were one of the bodies looted by the veteran from the Fort Craig cemetery. The vandal was proud of his actions and would boast about them to those who would listen. Charges were brought against the man but were dropped after his death. His home was said to be a "looter's paradise," as it was filled with Civil War artifacts.

Longest Inhabited New Mexico Forts

Above: Kit Carson would sit on the porch of the Officer's Quarters and have a great view of the Black Mesa and the Confederate troop movements near Fort Craig. *Courtesy of the author's collection.*

Right: The flagpole at Fort Craig's parade grounds is the tallest structure for miles. A soldier's daily life would have been centered on this pole. *Courtesy of the author's collection.*

Managed by the Bureau of Land Management, Fort Craig is a National Historic Site on El Camino Real de Tierra Adentro. *Courtesy of the author's collection.*

Directions and Information

Please be aware that some of the online instructions to Fort Craig have it located within the city limits of Socorro, New Mexico—these are incorrect; that is the field office location.

The Fort Craig National Monument is located thirty-five miles south of Socorro. If you are traveling from the north (from Albuquerque for example), take Interstate 25 to the San Marcial exit and then head south on old Highway 1 (which follows the same route as El Camino Real) for approximately eleven miles. Once you exit the highway, follow the signs to Fort Craig—the last part of the journey will be well-managed dirt roads.

If you are traveling from the south (from Las Cruces for example), take exit 115 off Interstate 25.

The fort is open year-round during daylight hours (it is only closed for Thanksgiving, Christmas and New Year's Day), and admission is free. There is a museum and gift shop on the site as well as clean restroom facilities and drinking water.

Fort Cummings (1846–1873)

Situated in present-day Luna County, New Mexico, among some of the most desolate vistas in the state, are the ruins of Fort Cummings. The largest saving grace of the fort was its proximity to Cooke's Spring, which was found, in 1846, by a Mormon Battalion on their way to California from Santa Fe, New Mexico during the Mexican-American War. The spring was the only water source for seventy to eighty miles around, and it was frequented by travelers, Native peoples and wildlife. The Mormon Battalion named the spring in honor of their commander, Colonel Philip St. George Cooke.

Fort Cummings was established by Captain Valentine Dresher, the commander of Company B of the First Infantry of the California Volunteers, on October 2, 1863. Although Cooke's Spring was used heavily for decades by travelers and passengers on the Butterfield Overland Mail Route and San Antonio–San Diego Mail and Passenger Services, the fort itself was not built until late 1863, during the Civil War. The construction of Fort Cummings took over a decade to complete, and due to the remoteness of its location, a small stage station had to be built within shooting distance of the fort to protect the soldiers and settlers from attacks.

The fort consisted of a hospital, officer's quarters, barracks and outer walls that were whitewashed. The twelve-foot-tall adobe walls and outer buildings were said to be void of windows and doors in order to dissuade Native attacks, but that statement was disproven by a photograph that included windows that appears on a sign at the site. An outer adobe wall and guard posts were built in 1867 by members of the Thirty-Eighth Infantry, Buffalo Soldiers. The fort would not have been easily breached by marauders. Taking this into account, the Apaches resorted to ambushes, which proved to be a highly successful and lethal method of attack.

Fort Cummings, located near Cooke's Spring in Southwest New Mexico, was a stronghold of protection for the wagon trains and mail routes. *Courtesy of the Library of Congress.*

Native Attacks

Fierce Apache chiefs, including Mangas Coloradas, Cochise, Victorio and Geronimo, called the western part of New Mexico home, and they were willing to defend their lands from the large groups of settlers, ranchers and miners who were invading them. Their defiance was the main reason the United States government established military forts in the western half of the New Mexico Territory. They were built to wage an all-out war against the Apache, and later, Navajo tribes.

In defense of the Apaches, Edwin R. Sweeney wrote in his work *Mangas Coloradas: Chief of the Chiricahua Apache*, "This major intrusion into the heart of Mangas Coloradas country not only destroyed the Apache land but also psychologically devastated the Indians." With the withdrawal of the army from New Mexico at the beginning of the Civil War, Mangas saw a perfect opportunity to rid his land of the invaders who were destroying it, and he waged war to drive out the Anglos and Hispanics who were left defenseless. It is thought more than four hundred travelers and settlers lost their lives around the Fort Cummings site.

After the construction of the fort, a cemetery was constructed in which to bury the people who had fallen victim to Native attacks; passengers on the Butterfield stagecoaches were complaining about the sight of sun-bleached skeletons littered along the route. Many of these victims were buried where they were found, which is why so many individual graves can be found along the trail leading to the fort. The valley through which the stages traveled along the Jornada del Muerto (Journey of Death), which stretches ninety miles through the New Mexico Territory, soon became known as Massacre

Valley, since it had very little shelter, water and food. It is thought that most of the bones gathered by the soldiers were buried with honors in a single grave, as was the tradition, since the ground was unforgiving and rocky.

One memorable battle involved the Freeman Thomas mail party in 1861, at the beginning of the Civil War and two years before the establishment of Fort Cummings. Thomas was a conductor on the San Antonio–San Diego Mail line who traveled the dangerous trails daily. Rumors of Mangas Coloradas and Cochise joining forces with a combined force of two hundred warriors sent chills through the seasoned stage driver. Preparing for the worst, Thomas supplied his wagon with as many arms as he could carry, including the all-important Sharps rifles and plenty of ammunition. As his coach entered Cooke's Canyon, in the shadow of the 8,400-foot-tall Cooke's Peak, an ambush had already been set up by the Apaches.

The battle that followed was said to have been one of the fiercest ever fought between Natives and settlers at the time. Taking a high and defensive

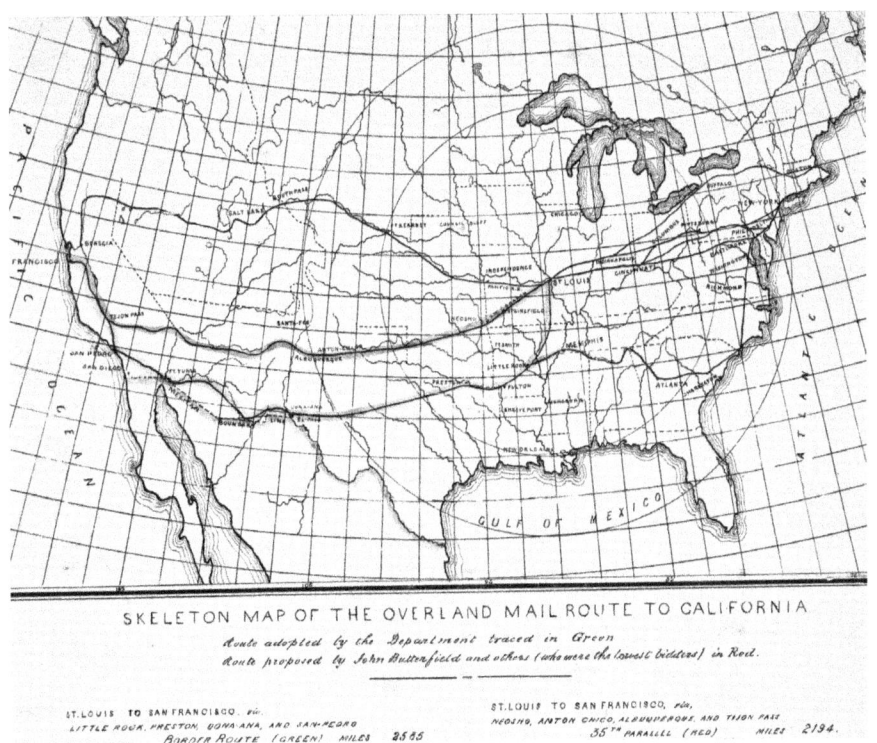

Overland mail routes crisscrossed the United States and were a constant target for attack by Native tribes. *Courtesy of the Library of Congress.*

stand, Thomas and his drivers fought off the attack for two days. When it seemed all was lost, they unhitched their team of horses from the wagon and sent them down the hill in the hopes the Natives would follow them, giving the drivers a chance to make their escape. The Apache lost twenty-five warriors in the fight, and when they eventually took over the small band of drivers, they took their revenge by mutilating the bodies of the men and leaving them in the hot summer sun. When passing freighters happened upon the horrible scene, the intensity of the battle was evident from the enormous amount of spent rifle casings that were scattered on the ground. These men certainly did not die without putting up a fight. Cochise was said to have been extremely impressed by the skills of his opponents and said, "If I had twenty-five fighters like Thomas and his men, I would undertake to whip the whole United States."

The fierce determination of the Apache leaders drew the attention of the Lincoln administration. Although his administration was deeply embroiled in the Civil War, it saw the great need to have a military presence in New Mexico in order to protect those settlers left behind. Soldiers dispatched from Fort Cummings spent most of their time following the tribes in the surrounding mountains, but they rarely encountered them. The fort was later abandoned in 1873, but it was reoccupied in 1880 after the escape of Chief Victorio from the San Carlos Reservation. After his escape, he threatened the southern and western regions of New Mexico and continued his crusade against the invaders of his lands. Fort Cummings would remain open until the surrender of Geronimo at Skeleton Canyon in southwestern New Mexico in 1886, which was the end the Apache Wars.

Buffalo Soldiers

As with other forts in the New Mexico Territory, the Buffalo Soldiers played a huge role in the protection of Fort Cummings and provided manual labor in the construction of its adobe buildings. The Buffalo Soldiers also worked in conjunction with the Indian Scouts, who were employed by the United States Army. The scouts were often paid in paper money, which they had no true understanding of, and would often be taken advantage of by the sutlers and store owners in the area. Because of this, fort commanders started paying scouts with a commodity more familiar to them—silver dollars.

Adobe bricks, made from clay, dirt and straw, were the preferred building materials for many New Mexico forts. *Courtesy of the Library of Congress.*

Fort Cummings Today

A few of the adobe ruins of Fort Cummings dot the desolate site today; remnants of a hospital building and the Cooke Spring's Wellhouse now sit on land owned by the Bureau of Land Management. Although there is a large amount of debris scattered around the site, such as old tin cans, bottles and ceramic shards, it is illegal to pick these items up.

Evidence of ancient civilizations have been found in Cooke's Canyon in the form of petroglyphs. These glyphs are believed to be over three thousand years old, and they are carved into the volcanic rocks scattered around the canyon.

Accessible only by four-wheel drive vehicles on a rough road, Fort Cummings sits as a dismal shadow of its former self, which was once described as being the best-looking fort in the territory. It is deteriorating with every rainstorm that graces the isolated plains; soon, it may be completely forgotten by history.

Directions

From Deming, take Highway 180 toward Silver City. Turn right at exit 41 on the Hatch Highway NE or County Road 26 and then turn left on Cooke's Canyon Road NE, past Flying U Road NE, and continue straight for approximately five miles. The ruins of the fort will be in sight.

FORT MARCY (1846–1868)

All that remains of Fort Marcy, the once proud fortress that protected New Mexico's capital city of Santa Fe, is a dirt mound on a hill overlooking the sprawling "City Different." It was the first United States Army post established in the southwestern region of the country, and from its vantage point, Fort Marcy provided a perfect view of possible attacks from all sides.

On August 18, 1846, during the Mexican-American War, General Stephen Watts Kearny, who was known as the "father of the United States Cavalry," marched into Santa Fe with over 1,600 men (also known as the Army of the West), captured the small Hispanic village and raised the American flag in the Santa Fe Plaza. The sitting commanding general and Mexican governor, Manuel Armijo, requested help from his people in the face of invasion, but he eventually decided not to resist, and Santa Fe was taken without a shot. The occupation of Santa Fe by the Army of the West provided a much-needed boost to the local economy from the opening of the Santa Fe Trail and the fur trade. It is said Colonel Edwin V. Sumner once referred to Santa Fe as "a sink of vice and extravagance." As the oldest state capital in the United States, Santa Fe is still known worldwide for its high-class lifestyle and expensive cost of living.

Fort Marcy, which was first built next to the Palace of the Governors, was commissioned by General Kearny to be built by his chief engineers: Lieutenants Jeremy Gilmer and William Emory. They chose a spot on a hill that was approximately 650 yards due northeast from the Santa Fe Plaza. The men began to build the fort using sun-dried adobe bricks; they eventually created five-foot-thick, nine-foot-high walls in a hexagonal shape that were surrounded by deep *acequias* (ditches). Since the fort was built using the rammed-earth method, soldiers were instructed to carry buckets of water up the one-hundred-foot-high embankment to moisten

Longest Inhabited New Mexico Forts

Fort Marcy met its demise in 1887, when $2,300 worth of gold coins was found buried on the site and treasure hunters brought its walls down. *Courtesy of the Library of Congress.*

the layered, sandy soil of the walls. After each layer, the soil was compacted by the feet of the troops who would walk along the top of the adobe walls. Archaeologists have found the adobe bricks contained bits of broken pottery, worked stones and even leftover corn cobs—which they believed belonged to the ancient inhabitants. Wood was such a rarity at Fort Marcy it is reported the soldiers and townsfolk would break up wagon boxes to make coffins when needed.

Initially, the sole purpose of the fort was to show military strength, as it was built high on a hill above the village below—literally within firing range of anything in sight. The American flag was raised quickly so that there would be no doubt about who was in charge. This site was no stranger to conflict—it saw many struggles between the occupational forces that had inhabited since ancient times. Although Fort Marcy was only intended to be temporary, it was considered the first army fort in the Southwest.

Right: Santa Fe Plaza has been the heart of New Mexico's capital city for nearly four hundred years and is a National Historic Landmark. *Courtesy of the Library of Congress.*

Below: Fort Marcy was built 650 yards from the center of Santa Fe, New Mexico, and housed over 1,700 troops. *Courtesy of the Library of Congress.*

The namesake of the fort was William L. Marcy, the secretary of war at the time of the fort's construction. Grand plans were drawn up for Fort Marcy that included blueprints for soldiers' quarters. The quarters were meant to hold up to 280 men when they were complete, but they never materialized. Kearny only planned for quarters because he was expecting much more resistance from the citizens of Santa Fe than he actually received. In fact, he met so little resistance that his men and horses were allowed to take up quarters next to the Palace of the Governors on the Plaza without any incident.

Fort Marcy saw no action during the Civil War, but it was at the ready in case another revolt were to occur. Due to the fact it was not needed, the fort was eventually abandoned in August 1868. The adobe walls of the fort were soon reclaimed by nature and by the villagers, who took the bricks to reinforce their own structures. The final destruction of the military fortress came when a local citizen reported that they had found a large cache of Spanish gold coins hidden in one of the walls of the fort. Treasure hunters from nearby territories converged on Santa Fe, digging around the old fort until it was destroyed completely.

After being sold at auction in 1891 by the United States government, the site was not owned again by the city of Santa Fe until 1961, when it was turned into a city park.

Fort Marcy Today

Situated on the road to Hyde Park, Fort Marcy could be missed easily by those unaware of its existence. Behind the Fort Marcy Condominiums, there is a quiet parking lot that looks over the City Different. This location was said, by the engineers, to be "the only point which commands the entire town." The Fort Marcy Suites now hold this location, and they also have a spectacular view of Santa Fe. The condominiums are a peaceful spot away from the hustle and bustle of the city, but they are close enough that the action of the city can be reached with a short walk.

All that is left of the fort today are dirt mounds that were once the foundations of the garrison walls. It is almost like the earth has reclaimed this fort and erased any evidence of its existence. A paved path with informative signs winds down from the fort ruins and ends at the Cross of the Martyrs, which can be seen from most locations in Santa Fe. The Cross of the Martyrs is a twenty-five-foot-tall steel cross monument that stands

Today, Fort Marcy consists of dirt mounds which once served as foundations for the adobe structures of the fort. *Courtesy of the author's collection.*

proudly overlooking the city below. This monument was erected in 1920 to commemorate the twenty-one Franciscan Friars who lost their lives during the bloody Pueblo Revolt of 1680. In years past, a fiesta and candlelight procession from Saint Francis Cathedral to the Cross of the Martyrs was held to celebrate the return of the Spaniards to the area, but this practice has been discontinued in recent years.

Today, a nearby park named for the fort is used for one of Santa Fe's most unique events—the burning of Old Man Gloom, or, as he is known to locals, Zozobra. This tradition began in 1924, when local artist Will Shuster decided to emulate the similar celebrations of the Yaqui Indians in Mexico. From 1924 to 1963, Shuster built a fifty-foot-tall, working marionette in the image of the bogeyman every year until he assigned all rights and interest over to the Kiwanis Club, who continue his vision as a fundraising event. When September rolls around each year, residents and visitors begin to fill up the "gloom box," which is located in the offices of the *Santa Fe Reporter*, with slips of paper that have their troubles, worries or negative thoughts written on them. The highlight of the Fiestas de Santa Fe is the burning of the gruesome puppet, which is stuffed with these slips of paper. Each year, the event draws over fifty thousand spectators who wish to witness their

Above: Cross of the Martyrs, located at the Fort Marcy site, commemorates the martyrdom of the priests who were killed on the hill. *Courtesy of the author's collection.*

Left: The burning of Zozobra, or Old Man Gloom, is a Santa Fe tradition that draws in many tourists to the area. *Courtesy of the author's collection.*

negativity go up in literal smoke. The moaning and wailing sound effects emanating from the marionette can give spectators goosebumps, but once Old Man Gloom is completely consumed by the flames, a great cheer is given out by the attendees, and the festivities begin.

Directions

Located in the heart of Santa Fe, the Fort Marcy ruins can be accessed by taking Washington Avenue three blocks north, which will intersect Paseo De Peralta at a light. Continue straight across Paseo De Peralta (Washington Avenue will become Bishops Lodge Road), turn right on Artist Road and follow it for two blocks (Artist Road will become Hyde Park Road). When you turn right onto Prince Avenue, the historical site will be to the left of the Fort Marcy Condominiums.

FORT SELDEN (1865–1890)

The once stately adobe walls of the southernmost fort along the Rio Grande are beginning to decay with time, but Fort Selden State Monument is working to preserve the last remnants of the Civil War–era fortress. North of the Robledo Mountains, Fort Selden is part of the Radium Springs community, which is thirteen miles north of Las Cruces, New Mexico, in the Rio Grande Valley. This fertile valley was once home to the ancient Mogollon tribe, who called the region home from AD 400 to the 1300s, when they melded with the northern Puebloan people. Evidence of their existence is found on the historical site; dome-shaped pit houses, fire pits and pottery that have been unearthed give modern-day residents a glimpse into the ways of these ancient people.

Built by soldiers from Albuquerque in May 1865, Fort Selden stood in defense of the southwestern region of what was then the Arizona Territory. The fort was named for Colonel Henry R. Selden of the First New Mexico Infantry, who was born in Vermont. It originally quartered two companies of men: one infantry, Company C of the First California Infantry, and one cavalry, Company M of the First California Cavalry.

Fort Selden was then home to the men of the 125th Infantry and 9th Cavalry, who were best known as the Buffalo Soldiers. Fort Selden was

A vintage image of the rock foundations of the soldiers' quarters at Fort Selden shows the attention to detail taken in construction. *Courtesy of the Library of Congress.*

An example of a United States Army supply wagon in a setting similar to everyday life at Fort Selden. *Courtesy of the author's collection.*

culturally diverse and represented many heritages of the region, including those of African Americans, European Americans, Hispanics and Native Americans. For some of the soldiers, Fort Selden was the first exposure to the harsh environment of the Southwest desert; luckily for them, the harshness of the desert was eased by the fort's proximity to the Rio Grande and the nearby mineral hot springs, known today as Radium Springs.

Description of Fort Selden

The significance of Fort Selden was lauded by Major J.C. McFerras in his 1865 "Annual Report of the Quartermaster General." It is located at an elevation of 4,250 feet, twenty-five miles west of the majestic Organ Mountains and four miles east of Picacho Peak. The surrounding forts are a good distance away from Fort Selden: Fort McRae is fifty-eight miles away, Fort Cummings is fifty-five miles away and Fort Bliss, in Texas, is sixty-seven miles away. Nearby Leasburg provided the fort's soldiers with entertainment and supplies.

Early reports describe the fort as being built on sandy soil that covered volcanic rocks. Much of New Mexico was formed by volcanic activity, the evidence of which can be found throughout the landscape. There are at least twenty-five documented volcanoes in the state that are between 9 million and 40,000 years old, and they produced lava flows, primarily in the western section of the state, only 5,200 years ago. Continued volcanic activity is also evident by the presence of the hot springs (first named Indian Hot Springs, now known as Radium Springs) near the fort. The many hot springs in the region near Fort Selden were highly prized and readily used by Native tribes and settlers, who used them for washing clothes and bathing.

Although there is a debate over the original location of the fort, early plans reveal that Fort Selden was meant to replace the smaller outposts, like Fort Cummings, Fort Conrad, Fort McRae and Fort Thorn in New Mexico, as well as Forts Bowie and Grants in Arizona. The expansion of Fort Selden, from a single adobe building, which housed two hundred men, was said to have cost $251,451.69 in 1872. After the expansion, the fort was able to house twelve companies of soldiers and cover 9,613.74 acres of land. The expansion was championed by Brevet Major General John Pope, the commander of the headquarters of the Department of Missouri, who wrote a letter to the secretary of war, Robert T. Lincoln, in which he stated: "Experience has made it manifest that the large military interest will be best served by the establishment of one large post to replace several smaller posts in that region of the country."

The arid environment, which consisted of cottonwood trees (many of which are still in place), spiny mesquite bushes and prickly cacti was a shock for most of the soldiers stationed at Fort Selden. Most of them came from the Midwest and eastern states to a fort that was once described in the 1870 Surgeon General's Report:

> [It] *must have been unbearable in the summer months when the temperatures ran close to the century mark during the day. Adobe dormitories with three to four-foot thick walls, which keep the structure cool, were most definitely a welcomed reprieve for the soldiers, even without ventilation. Many reports also state there were "annoyingly numerous wolves and skunks around the post."*

Water had to be hauled daily from the Rio Grande, and it had to be left to "settle" with charcoal due to the high amount of mud. It is estimated that, at the time, mud made up 95 percent of the "water" the soldiers pulled from the river. Since the Rio Grande ran full during the spring runoff, a rope ferry was in operation between one and one and a half miles above the post, and it was used mainly by the local citizens and soldiers to safely ferry animals and supplies through the floodwaters to Fort Selden and surrounding homesteads.

Conditions at Fort Selden were far from ideal, but they were not as bad as they were at other forts. Enlisted men could bring their families to the area if they were married—the thought behind this allowance was that the families would have a calming effect on the men and keep them from gambling and drinking. Nearby Leasburg was enticing to the men, since it provided dancing, drinking, women and gambling. This entertainment also created a dangerous situation, which saw up to eight men from the fort lose their lives in fights with the locals.

The women at the forts were instrumental in establishing a bit of culture in the wilderness around every fort in which they lived. Churches and schools were built to accommodate the needs of the forts. The United States government passed a law in the 1880s that stated all children of enlisted men had to attend school and the children of officers had to be privately tutored or schooled in the eastern part of the nation. The quality of education provided at the forts was thought to be inefficient by most, since teachers were scarce.

A government-issued Remington Model 1863 pistol was one of the most important firearms in the American West. It was carried by outlaws, soldiers and frontiersmen for protection. *Courtesy of the author's collection.*

In order to develop a more home-like environment, the ladies of the fort would coordinate and cook elaborate meals on special occasions, such as Christmas or Thanksgiving, to circumvent homesickness—supplies were minimal and not as sanitary during the rest of the year. The post surgeon wrote in his 1870 report:

> *I have carefully inspected and tested all varieties of flour on hand. The best, that from Socorro, contain weavils [sic], bugs, and worms, and have lumps of various sizes. An average of more than ten pounds of this stuff is sieved from each sack.*

Two interesting examples of fort recipes are on display at the Fort Selden Museum:

Artillery Pie (Sufficient for 22 men)
8 pounds bread
4 dozen apples
1 pound suet
2 pounds sugar

Melt the suet in a frying pan, cut the bread into slices one-quarter of an inch in thickness, dip each in the melted fat, and place them in an oven to dry. In the meanwhile, get the apples peeled, boiled and mashed with sugar. Cover the bottom of the baking dish with the bread, cover the bread with some apples, then some more bread over that, then the apples, thus until all is used; place in an oven and bake for twenty minutes.

Cannon Balls (Sufficient for 22 men)
6 pounds flour
1½ pounds suet
3 pints molasses
1 pint water

Chop up the suet, mix with flour, mix the molasses with water, put the flour (hopefully, bug free) into a bowl, pour the molasses gradually upon it, mixing it with the flour; when the whole is well mixed, and not too soft, form it into any size balls required, flour some cloths, tie up each ball separately in cloth, not too tight, and boil from one hour upward, according to size.

These, with lime juice, are an excellent antiscorbutic, and will keep good for twelve months, and longer. They could be made before going on any long voyage and given out as rations.

Rations at the fort generally consisted of flour, salt pork, beans and coffee, but the sutlers of the fort were able to supply a few of the more exotic ingredients of the recipes, such as molasses and apples, through trade with the locals.

In the Shadow of Robledo Mountain

The Sombre Robledo Mountain was named after a sixteenth-century nobleman, Don Pedro Robledo, who accompanied Don Juan de Oñate to New Spain, now known as New Mexico, in 1598. Due to the presence of highwaymen and thieves, who used the mountain as a haven, Charles III of Spain ordered dragoons from Santa Fe to the post, along with men from Juarez, to protect and escort the travelers along the Jornada del Muerto. Their quarters were said to consist of "barracks of upright poles checkered

Robledo Mountain proudly rises to the south of Fort Selden and was home to many of the local Native tribes. *Courtesy of the author's collection.*

with adobe." History vaguely hints at the possibility of a Spanish fort being built in the same vicinity as Fort Selden, but concrete proof has been extremely difficult to obtain. There is proof that a mule station did exist at the base of the mountain during the time of Spanish settlement; it was occupied by Confederate soldiers, who wrote about being stationed at Robledo Camp, in 1861.

Although it has long been thought of as a cantankerous animal, the mule quickly proved to be one of the best tools soldiers could have with them, especially in the desolate, arid deserts of southwestern New Mexico, where Fort Selden and other forts were located, because of their stamina and ability to travel long distances. There is evidence of the offspring of a female horse and a male donkey being bred in Egypt as far back as before 3000 BC, and one of the first American breeders was George Washington. Since mules were much less expensive to purchase than horses, the United States Army was able to employ over one million of the stubborn beasts into service during the Civil War. Mules are tough and strong but have sensitive ears that do not take well to gun or cannon fire. The commotion often triggered a self-preservation mode in the animals, causing them to bolt. In these scenarios, the horse was better suited.

With the ability to eat just about anything, from cacti and scrub oak to leather, the mule had an advantage over horses during long treks through the barren desert. According to an 1867 book written by muleskinner-turned-author Harry Riley, the mule was an admirable, misunderstood creature.

> *There is no more useful or willing animal than the mule. And perhaps there is no other animal so much abused, or so little cared for. Popular opinion of his nature has not been favorable; and he has had to plod and work through life against the prejudices of the ignorant.*

Unfortunately, horses and mules were often the innocent victims in war; they did their jobs as well as any human soldier, but they were considered expendable. According to estimates from historians, in the Battle of Gettysburg alone, over 43,303 horses and 21,844 mules were killed or wounded and left for dead. Once the battle commenced, the carcasses

The mule was one of the best accessories used by the United States Army due to its calm temperament and surefootedness. *Courtesy of the Library of Congress.*

of dead animals littered the landscape, and all of them needed to be buried or disposed of correctly. It was decided that, since the burial of the one-thousand-pound animals was too labor-intensive, they would be burned. Memoirs of citizens who lived in the area tell of the awful stench of burning horseflesh that smelled like "an escape from a hateful charnal house." (A charnal house is a vault used to contain the bones of humans, a house of death and destruction.) There were efforts to save some of the minorly wounded animals, but if they were eventually deemed unable to be of benefit to the army or civilians, they were also shot.

Famous Faces

The MacArthurs were some of the most famous people that ever resided at Fort Selden. The Fort Selden Museum has a photo of young Douglas MacArthur, who was born in 1880, posing with his family; Fort Seldon's staff have affectionately dubbed the young boy with long hair and short pants "Dougie." Although he was a young boy during his stay at Fort Selden, MacArthur said that he learned to shoot and ride before he could read or write and that enjoyed his three years at the fort in the New Mexico Territory.

Arthur MacArthur moved his wife, Mary (Pinky), and three sons, Arthur III, Malcolm and Douglas, to the New Mexico Territory when he assumed post command of the fort in 1884 after being transferred from Fort Wingate. Under his command, the soldiers of Fort Selden, who were the members of Company K that consisted of forty-six enlisted men, a post surgeon and two officers, would participate in the campaign against the Apache war chief Geronimo.

Douglas's mother, Mary, took on the task of educating her sons, teaching only the most rudimentary skills. She also instilled a strong sense of obligation in the boys—they were to do what was right, no matter the personal sacrifice. Douglas took this education to heart and went on to become a five-star general.

Before the outbreak of the Civil War, the United States government began to look for an alternative to horses, which were expensive. One idea it came up with was to utilize camels in the deserts of the New Mexico Territory, Texas and Arizona. In 1859, an expedition of twenty-four camels and twenty-four mules set out on a 114-mile-long journey that stretched from the New Mexico Territory to Fort Stockton in Texas. It was concluded that the camels were far superior to the mules when they were able to continue

Five-star general Douglas MacArthur lived at Fort Selden as a young child, and it was also where he learned to shoot and ride. *Courtesy of the Library of Congress.*

to Fort Davis, Texas without distress, which was something the mules were unable to do. The experiment lost steam near the end of the Civil War, in 1864, when most of the animals were sold at auction—others were released into the desert. One of the released camels caused a panic at Fort Selden during an encounter with the young Douglas MacArthur.

One afternoon, the young boy was exploring the countryside surrounding the fort when a fearsome beast appeared out of the sagebrush, giving him a terrifying start. Douglas screamed at the top of his lungs. His mother and the rest of the fort, fearing the worst, an Indian attack, rushed to the rescue of the boy. When they found him, he was just a few feet away from a rogue camel. Not wanting to upset the commander's son, the soldiers shooed the creature away and escorted the child back to the arms of his worried mother. The story of this incident provided a good deal of entertainment at the camp for many years.

One of the greatest facts about Fort Selden is that it was home to five soldiers who were presented with the highest honor in the armed forces: the Congressional Medal of Honor. The soldiers received their honors following a battle with the Apaches between the dates of July 8 and 14, 1873. These men were Corporal Frank Bratling, Sergeant Leonidas S. Lytle, First Sergeant James Morris, Private Henry Willis and Company Blacksmith John Sheerin (all members of the Eighth Cavalry, Company C). Although little is written about the engagement, the details from the report sent by Captain George W. Chilson of Troop C, Eighth Cavalry, read:

> *Left post with ten mounted men on 9 Jul ultimo chasing Indians who had stolen horses from Shedd's Ranch. After following them for 4½ days, caught them west of Cañada Alamosa. I report the loss of Corporal Frank Bratling. Three Indians killed. The stock recovered. Distance covered 350 miles.*

Since he was the only one killed, Corporal Bratling was the only soldier in the group to be awarded the medal posthumously. They all received their medals on August 12, 1872.

To Abandon or Not to Abandon

Almost as soon as the expensive expansion of Fort Selden was complete, in October 1875, rumors of its abandonment began to swirl. In a telegraph from the chief signal officer of the army to the adjutant general of the army, a question was raised about whether Fort Selden was to be abandoned. This question was referred to General Pope, who responded that he was indeed planning on abandoning the fort "as soon as the last detachment of the North Cavalry passes there, going north." However, he also said, "I shall leave a guard."

Longest Inhabited New Mexico Forts

The ruins of the MacArthur quarters at Fort Selden are a reminder of the humble beginnings of the leader's life. *Courtesy of the author's collection.*

After concerns were raised by the citizens of Mesilla, New Mexico, in 1877, many letters from members of the War Department on the fate of Fort Selden were sent from 1877 to 1879, which manically ping-ponged back and forth. In numerous reports penned by General Pope starting in 1875, he states he would "gladly abandon Fort Selden," and he issued Special Order 32,9878 to begin this process. Through Special Order No. 52, Fort Selden was officially in an abandoned state as of May 1879. The same order also placed the fort under the jurisdiction of the commanding general of Fort Bliss in Texas. Special Order No. 144, dated December 25, 1880, requested the post be reoccupied by New Mexico troops. The last Special Order, No. 81, dated August 23, 1890, from the headquarters Department of Arizona, named Fort Selden as a subpost for Fort Bayard near Silver City, New Mexico, and a small number of troops were retained there until 1892.

Once the fort was abandoned, the roofs, windows and doors were removed, which, unfortunately, led to the rapid destruction of the adobe walls of the fort buildings.

Fort Selden Today

Today, the fort is amid rich farmland, with a prosperous winery across the street, which also bears the Fort Selden name. The adobe remains of the fort are in a precarious condition, and the historic walls must be braced with lumber to prevent them from falling over. Students from New Mexico State University History Department are working diligently to restore the ruins, fighting a brilliant fight against time and the elements.

The Fort Selden site offers an informative museum, a short video on the history of the fort and an easy walking tour featuring seventeen stops. The walking tour guide provides great insight to the historic features along the walk. Living history demonstrations are also available on the weekends from 1 p.m. to 4 p.m. from May 1 to September 15. Special programming also occurs throughout the year, and information about that can be found on their website.

The rattlesnake warning sign at Fort Selden may be humorous, but rattlesnakes are dangerous and need to be taken seriously. *Courtesy of the author's collection.*

Since the fort is in a desert setting, there is wildlife present, including rattlesnakes. The fort staff asks for visitors to be wary of the reptiles, since they tend to blend in with the vegetation. Visitors should be sure to give them a wide berth and to not agitate them in any way, since they are venomous.

If you can, please help with the preservation efforts. This fort will not be available for future generations to enjoy without your help and generosity.

Directions and Information

Fort Selden is thirteen miles north of Las Cruces, New Mexico, in Radium Springs. Follow Interstate 25 north to Albuquerque, Exit 19. Turn right at Exit 19, and then turn left to go over the bridge that crosses Interstate 25. Continue along that road for approximately three miles; the historical site will be on the right.

The Sentinel, a statue by New Mexico sculptor Reynaldo Rivera, honors the Ninth Cavalry Buffalo Soldiers as he keeps watch over Fort Selden, New Mexico. *Courtesy of the author's collection.*

1280 Fort Selden Road
Radium Springs, New Mexico 88054

It is recommended to call the Visitor's Center and Museum ahead of your visit to make sure the site is open. The center's number is (575) 526-8911.

Hours:
The fort is open from 8:30 a.m. to 5:00 p.m., Wednesday through Sunday. The admission fee is five dollars. Admission is free to New Mexico residents (with a valid ID) on the first Sunday of every month to New Mexico seniors (with a valid ID) on Wednesdays.

FORT STANTON (1855–PRESENT)

Established in 1855 by order of General John Garland, Fort Stanton is one of the most fascinating forts in New Mexico. Named for Captain Henry Stanton, who was killed in an ambush on January 19, 1855 by Mescalero Apaches, the fort was used in defense of the settlers who were homesteading along the Rio Bonito. In 1896, the fort was established as an Indian Agency for the Apaches, who were rounded up by American soldiers.

The fort's central location, 240 acres on the banks of the Rio Bonito, between the historic towns of Lincoln and Capitan, was in the best situation for the mission given to its troops: eradicate the Mescalero Apaches. The Mescalero Apaches were a nomadic tribe who claimed a large swath of land as theirs and fought hard to keep it from falling into the settlers' hands. The United States government did not share the same passion, so it assembled troops at the fort for the sole purpose of eliminating the "pests," as they were referred to in the soldiers' reports. Members of the tribe who refused to stay on the reservation were hunted and, in some cases, killed.

Fort Stanton was also a prize for the invading Confederate army due to its location. When the Confederate army advanced on the fort, Union troops were ordered to set it ablaze so as to not leave anything of value for the Confederates to use. Mother Nature took it upon herself to save the fort by bringing a rainstorm to extinguish the flames—the Confederates took over the burned buildings. Kit Carson and his New Mexico Volunteers reclaimed the fort one year later, in 1862, under the orders of General James Carleton. During the recapturing of the fort, Carson was also ordered to exterminate

Longest Inhabited New Mexico Forts

Mescalero Apache teepees were made from wood and covered with tanned buffalo or elk hides. The tipis were set up by the women of the tribe. *Courtesy of the Library of Congress.*

any male Apache he saw and to capture the women and children. Over four hundred Mescalero Apache surrendered to Carson at Fort Stanton, and going against orders, the frontiersman allowed the men to live. While Carson could have been court-martialed for this offense, he had no charges filed against him.

Carson's captives, and others later obtained, would meet a fate that would become known as one of the worst experiments in United States history. More can be read about the Long Walk and the Bosque Redondo in the Fort Sumner section, as it was from Fort Stanton that Carson and his troops captured hundreds of Mescalero Apaches who were then sent to the Bosque Redondo at Fort Sumner in 1862 and 1863. When the Mescalero finally escaped their horrendous prison at Fort Sumner, the Buffalo Soldiers were sent to Fort Stanton to round up the escapees. Through their efforts in the years following 1865, the tribe was said to be under control and docile by 1871.

It is also said that the outlaw William H. Bonney, who was also known as Billy the Kid, spent some time in the fort's stockade after haunting the Fort Stanton region. He was in the fort awaiting his hanging, but this event never occurred. He died at a private home at Fort Sumner, in 1881. During a famous gunfight between Captain Paddy Graydon and the company doctor, John Whitlock, who had accused Graydon of massacring a peaceful band of Mescalero Apaches, Graydon was under the extermination orders of General Carleton, which were the same orders as those given to Carson. Although the doctor received a nonlethal gunshot wound, he did not survive; Graydon's men took their revenge for the mortal wound Graydon had received at Whitlock's hand.

Buffalo Soldiers

While stationed at Fort Stanton, the primary role of the Buffalo Soldier was to help in the eradication of the local Mescalero Apache tribe who lived in the surrounding White and Sacramento Mountains. The soldiers also aided local lawmen in Lincoln County in issuing warrants, and they were a show a force during the Lincoln County War. As with other forts where the Buffalo Soldiers were stationed, they were put to work rebuilding the burned-out structures and building new ones on the site.

Lincoln County War

Fort Stanton and the Mescalero Apache Reservation were the largest consumers of beef in Lincoln County, which ultimately lead to the famed Lincoln County War. A feud between the Murphy-Dolan gang and the Tunstall faction resulted in the five-day battle in Lincoln, New Mexico. In the height of the battle, troops were sent in from Fort Stanton, under the command of Colonel Nathan Dudley, to only be a neutral military show. This all changed when a gung-ho commander decided to choose sides by setting the house of attorney Alexander McSween on fire. Dudley's action of turning a blind eye to this display of aggression resulted in the deaths of four men, including McSween.

Once the Indian Wars came to a halt, Fort Stanton once again returned to being a near ghost town, with only fifteen soldiers stationed there in 1893. Ultimately, the fort was officially decommissioned in 1896. Fort Stanton would not languish for long, as the United States Public Health Service acquired the property to be used as a Merchant Marine hospital for the treatment of tuberculosis. The fort served over 5,000 patients between 1899 and 1953, and it would later be known as the Public Health Service Hospital. The Maritime Cemetery holds over 1,500 of these patients within its walls.

Lincoln County Courthouse was a witness to the Lincoln County War, the exploits of Billy the Kid, and is now a part of the Lincoln Historic Site. *Courtesy of the Southeastern New Mexico Historical Society.*

Tuberculosis

As the ravages of tuberculosis, or "the grip," tore across the United States, the mild climate of New Mexico was welcomed as a perfect place for victims to recover. Tuberculosis centers popped up across the territorial landscape to service the multitudes of sufferers who flocked to the region seeking treatment and, they hoped, a cure. Many communities in southeastern and central New Mexico played host to tubercular patients who had basically come to the state to die. The recovery rate astounded doctors, as the patients literally lived in specially constructed tents in the open air and worked on the nearby farms as a form of therapy. Recreation was available as well, with a golf course for the doctors and a theater and baseball fields for the patients.

Internment Camps

Fort Stanton played host to the Civil Conservation Corps (CCC), which had a work camp on site, and it served as a source for refuge for several Japanese American families who were being brutalized by mobs in their hometowns. There were a few Japanese citizens held at the fort for a short time, but the best-known foreign residents of Fort Stanton were the German prisoners of war.

In 1939, the crew of the SS *Columbus*, a German luxury liner, under strict orders from Hitler, scuttled their ship, as capture by a British warship seemed eminent. The crew was rescued off the coast of New York, which immediately posed a problem to the United States government—what was it going to do with these noncombatants? The crew was first sent to San Francisco, California, but the United States government felt the area was too recognizable to the men, so it was decided that the small Civil War–era fort in the middle of the New Mexico central mountains would be a far better home for this naval group.

Fort Stanton's scenic location boded well for the German crew, who were mainly musicians. The prisoners were allowed many luxuries in their new home, such as access to the Sears catalogue, from which they could order seeds for their gardens. Many of the men had their own cottages that were surrounded by the flowers and vegetables they planted. The fruits of their labor were often taken to the nearby towns and sold to the citizens for extra spending money for the prisoners. During their internment, the Olympic Games were held in Germany, so the prisoners dug and built an Olympic-sized swimming pool in which they held their own games; remnants of this pool still exists today. Movie night was also a regular form of entertainment for the prisoners; it was held outside and a projector displayed the images on the side of the mess hall. Life was much better for these men in the United States than it was for their American counterparts in Germany. Although life was good in the camp, there were a couple of escape attempts, but the prisoners learned quickly that navigating the mountains was far more difficult than it appeared. They were always easily captured and returned.

Toward the end of World War II, another camp was set up a bit farther east of the original. The prisoners at the new camp were Nazi sympathizers and not as genial as their countrymen. The camps were separated to ensure no collusion occurred, and residents and schoolchildren of the towns were warned not to reveal their location or show maps or books to the prisoners in order to keep their location a secret. Several of the

Fort Stanton POW camp was a pleasant place to be interned. It allowed many freedoms, and the inmates were well-treated by the guards and staff. *Courtesy of the author's collection.*

German POWs built a concrete pool, which they used for their own Olympic games at Fort Stanton. *Courtesy of the author's collection.*

Some of the German prisoners who were held at Fort Stanton during World War II asked to be buried in the fort's cemetery after their deaths. *Courtesy of the author's collection.*

original German crew members returned to the United States after the war and visited the fort again. Four crew members loved the location so much that they asked to be buried in the Fort Stanton Naval Cemetery. Permission was granted.

Fort Stanton after the World Wars

In 1953, the state of New Mexico had twenty-seven thousand acres of land transferred to it by the military, which included Fort Stanton so it could be used as a tuberculosis center until 1966. As the tuberculosis crisis waned, the fort's hospital was used as a training school for children with mental disabilities, under the New Mexico Department of Health, until 1995. The fort the became a minimum-security women's prison from 1996 to 1999, and minimal visitation was allowed, since it was also a youth drug rehabilitation center.

In 1997, Fort Stanton Inc. was formed to start restoration efforts on the historic fort with hopes of turning the site into a living history center. On August 9, 2007, Lieutenant Governor Diane Denish declared this historical treasure the Fort Stanton State Monument.

Fort Stanton Today

Fort Stanton is a proud reminder of the diverse history in New Mexico: people of Anglo-Saxon, Hispanic, Native and African American descent all occupied the fort during its tenure. Preservation efforts to maintain the many architectural styles that comprise the post are ongoing at the fort. The Friends of Fort Stanton strive to introduce the public to the rich history of the fort by hosting numerous events each year, including Fort Stanton Days (which corresponds with Billy the Kid Days in Lincoln), Fort Stanton After Dark and Fort Stanton Live (which is held every July). Admission fees for special events may apply.

During a restoration project at the fort, a stone was found under the exterior porch floor of the old administration building, which now houses the museum. "The Rock," as it is known, was inscribed with a crossed saber insignia—the symbol of the cavalry—and the year 1882. According to fort historians, there were four cavalry units at the fort in that particular year: Companies B, D, I and the Fourth U.S. Cavalry. It is also thought that the building housed troops from the Fourth Regiment. Another small rock was found imbedded in the doorstep of the building in the corral across the street. This rock was also carved with the year 1882. The carvings are thought to be a troop identifier, possibly belonging to the "Color Troop," which kept the unit's flags and streamers.

Another great feature of Fort Stanton is the Fort Stanton Snowy River Cave National Conservation Area, which includes the second-longest cave in New Mexico at just over thirty-one miles. Evidence was found in 2001 that even the soldiers at the fort enjoyed this beautiful cave. Should visitors want to explore the cave, they must first obtain a permit from the Bureau of Land Management (BLM) office in Roswell, New Mexico. It is also suggested that visitors call ahead, due to the fact the cave is closed intermittently to protect the resident bat population from disease.

The fort has partnered with the BLM to oversee the acreage and provide maintenance for the close to one hundred miles of hiking, biking and horseback riding trails and camp sites located within fort lands. As one of the most well-preserved forts in New Mexico, Fort Stanton boasts over fifty-three buildings in a breath-taking mountain location, which can be seen and explored by visitors. During your self-guided tour, stop under one of the majestic pine trees that line the parade grounds, close your eyes and take a moment to breathe in the history. You can almost hear the thud of horses' hooves on the ground and the clinks of saddle hardware as

Snowy River Cave is part of a 25,080-acre National Conservation Area established by Congress in 2009. The land also includes riding trails, campgrounds and shelters. *Courtesy of the author's collection.*

the soldiers of the past do maneuvers. Rumor has it that the fort may be haunted—so keep your eyes open for a ghostly soldier or two.

Some exciting discoveries have recently been made by preservationists working at the fort. A system of mortise and tenon joint rafters were found in the Commanding Officer's Quarters. The workers were reported as saying to the local newspaper, the *Ruidoso News*: "These joints were cut in about 1868 during the fort's reconstruction and [are] as tight as [they were] when [they were] made." The amazing construction used wooden pins to secure the joints and is a great testament to the craftsmanship of those who built it.

Directions and Information

To reach the Fort Stanton Historic Site, take Highway 380 out of Lincoln, New Mexico (Billy the Kid Scenic Trail), turn left on 220 (there will be signs) and follow the paved, two-lane road to the fort site at the Bonito River. The

Fort Stanton's Merchant Marine Cemetery is the final resting place for naval tubercular patients and soldiers. It is located next to Fort Stanton's Veteran Cemetery. *Courtesy of the author's collection.*

fort is situated between the towns of Lincoln and Capitan, New Mexico. You will be greeted with a stunning view of Sierra Blanca just before the turn-off.

Be sure to travel to the Fort Stanton Naval Cemetery a few miles past the fort site for another historical experience.

Fort Stanton
104 Kit Carson Road
Fort Stanton, NM 88323

For more information please call:
Visitor Center and Museum (575) 653-4372
Bureau of Land Management, Roswell Field Office: (575) 627-0272

Hours:
It is recommended that you call ahead, since they will close occasionally due to weather conditions.
The site is open daily from 8:00 a.m. to 5:00 p.m.
The museum is open daily from 10:00 a.m. to 4:00 p.m.
Admission is free.

Fort Sumner (1862–Present)

As the seat of De Baca County, the town of Fort Sumner served as a hub for commerce, medical care and agriculture for the far eastern reaches of the New Mexico Territory. In fact, when cattleman Oliver Loving, on whom the movie *Lonesome Dove* is loosely based, was ambushed by Apaches near present-day Carlsbad, he was taken to Fort Sumner for medical care. He would lose his battle and succumb to death before his friend, Charles Goodnight, also a part owner of the herd of cattle they were running at the time of the attack, could see him. Goodnight was then given the task of returning his friend's body back to his family in Texas. The Goodnight-Loving Cattle Trail is one of the most famous cattle trails in the Old West.

At the headwaters of the Pecos River, Fort Sumner was part of Manifest Destiny, which sought to corral and subdue the Native tribes of New Mexico, especially the *Dinè* (Navajo) and *N'de* (Mescalero Apaches), Comanches and Kiowas, who were the most troublesome in the area. The fort was the brainchild of James H. Carleton, who was a protégé of General Edwin Vose Sumner and also commanded the California Column. The services

The South Springs house was the headquarters of the Jingle-Bob Ranch and home to the largest cattle rancher in Southeast New Mexico, John Chisum. *Courtesy of the Southeastern New Mexico Historical Society.*

Fort Sumner, which was mainly built using adobe bricks, was washed completely away when the Pecos River changed its course and flooded the region in 1904. *Courtesy of the Southeastern New Mexico Historical Society.*

of the California Column were requested in the New Mexico Territory to counteract the Confederacy invasion, which was quickly moving up from the then-Confederate Arizona Territory and Texas.

After the Civil and Indian Wars, in 1869, Fort Sumner was abandoned and purchased by the largest land owner in the New Mexico Territory, Lucien Maxwell, who enlarged the officer's quarters to become his sprawling twenty-one-room home. It was at this home, in 1881, that Billy the Kid would meet his doom. Mrs. Lucien Maxwell and her son, Pete, disposed of the remaining fort buildings in 1884, and the fort fell to adobe ruins. It is unfortunate that the ruins of Fort Sumner were destroyed in the floods of 1921 and 1932.

Billy the Kid

Today, Fort Sumner's claim to fame centers on a popular, but controversial, character in New Mexico history: the outlaw William H. Bonney, who is more commonly known as Billy the Kid. Billy's short life ended in Fort

Sumner at the home of his good friend, Pete Maxwell on July 14, 1881. This fact is still being debated today.

During his career as a cowboy, Billy acquired the reputation of being an outlaw, gunslinger and all-around bad hombre. Was he as bad as they said? Probably not, but now there is no one left alive to dispute the accusations. Billy was said to be a fun-loving soul who was fluent in Spanish and Gaelic; he was also known to be lucky with the ladies and quite a good dancer. The local Hispanic population was known to enjoy Billy's company greatly, and they were extremely tight-lipped when asked about his location by lawmen.

The "luck of the Irish" did not seem to follow Billy, for he seemed to have some of the worst luck around, depending on perspective. The following are the events of Billy the Kid's short life in a nutshell.

It is thought by some historians that Billy started his life in New York City on November 23, 1859. He was born William Henry McCarty Jr., but not much else is known of his early life and childhood. His mother, Catherine McCarty, decided to move west, where it is thought she met William Antrim in Indianapolis, Indiana. The couple continued traveling and were married in Santa Fe, New Mexico, with Billy and his brother, Joseph, in attendance. The newlyweds then followed the gold trail to Silver City, New Mexico, where Antrim mined.

Tragically, Billy lost his mother in 1874 to tuberculosis, rendering him and his brother orphans at a young age. After her death, Billy and his brother were shuffled through foster homes, since his stepfather, William Antrim, showed no interest in raising the boys. Billy soon fell in with a rough crowd and under the influence of a petty thief by the name of Sombrero Jack. The Kid was arrested for stealing clothes from a Chinese laundry and thrown in jail. Being of small stature, the new outlaw was able to escape his cell by shimming up a chimney. Billy was then forced to move to Arizona to avoid the law, where it is said he committed his first murder in a saloon in 1877.

Billy returned to New Mexico as a cowboy who was proficient with a Winchester rifle and Colt revolver and went by the name William H. Bonney. While working for the largest cattle baron in the New Mexico Territory, John S. Chisum, the Kid was forced to rustle (or steal) cattle from his employer, who had refused to pay him. Chisum's ranch is said to have been 180 miles long, from north to south, and 100 miles wide, from east to west, beginning at Fort Sumner and ending at Seven Rivers (near Carlsbad) and held eighty thousand head of cattle. Billy was said to have taken his revenge out on the men who worked for Chisum by killing them when he found them, which sent a clear message to the cattleman. Chisum got Pat Garrett elected as Lincoln County sheriff for the sole intent of killing the Kid because of these thefts.

He then moved on to greener pastures and wound up in Lincoln County working for English cattleman John Tunstall, who had been encouraged to start his business in New Mexico by Captain Jack Hays. Tunstall treated the Kid well and developed a true brotherhood with the outlaw. The Englishman quickly made enemies with the Irishmen Lawrence J. Murphy and James J. Dolan, who ran the mercantile called the House across the street. When cattleman John S. Chisum and attorney Alexander McSween began to oppose the monopoly of the House, Tunstall joined in their efforts. Through an illegal court move, the House was able to win McSween and Tunstall's assets, which also sent Chisum to jail for a short time.

Although nonviolent, Tunstall was smart and surrounded himself with notorious gunfighters like Billy the Kid, Dick Brewer, John Middleton and Rob Widenmann. On the morning of February 18, 1878, a posse selected by the House was sent to Tunstall's ranch to confiscate his cattle. The Tunstall gunmen urged their employer not to confront the men, but he did not listen. Tunstall, who rode on horseback to speak with the posse, was shot down with a bullet to the chest. As he lay dying on the ground, another posse member finished the deed with a shot to the back of his head with the Englishman's own pistol.

Outlaw William H. Bonney went by many names, including Billy the Kid, but remains a beloved character in New Mexico folklore and history. *Courtesy of the Southeastern New Mexico Historical Society.*

After the brutal murder of Billy's close friend Tunstall, he set out to avenge his senseless death and was thrust into the middle of the Lincoln County War. During the five-day battle, Billy was accused of killing Sheriff

Brady in broad daylight as the lawman strode through the center of town on his morning rounds. Brady died from at least a dozen different gunshot wounds, but it was only Billy who was accused of the murder.

In 1879, reportedly at gunpoint, Billy and his compadre Tom O'Folliard were forced to witness the murder of Lincoln attorney Huston Chapman. The attorney was shot, and his body was set aflame in broad daylight on the streets of Lincoln. Billy started a letter-writing campaign to Governor Lew Wallace (who was also the author of *Ben Hur*) offering to give information about the heinous crime, reportedly committed by the outlaw Jesse Evans, in exchange for amnesty. The pair met secretly, and Governor Wallace promised the Kid protection in exchange for the information. Their plan was to have the Kid appear to be arrested for the crime, give testimony and be set free. Billy lived up to his part of the deal, but Sheriff Kimball refused to release him once his testimony was complete. Again, being of small stature, Billy was able to escape from the Lincoln County Courthouse on June 1, 1879. After betraying the trust of the Kid, Governor Wallace offered a $500 reward for Billy's capture on December 13, 1880, when he got word that the Kid had shot Joe Grant in Hargrove's Saloon in Fort Sumner. Pat Garrett, who was once a friend and co-worker of the Kid on the Chisum ranch, won the bid for Lincoln County sheriff, beating out Kimball, in 1880. Once he was sheriff, Garrett was given the sole task of hunting down and killing the Kid, a job that he seemed eager to accomplish, but the Kid was able to stay one step ahead of his old friend for many months.

Billy, along with gang members Tom Pickett, Dave "Dangerous Dave" Rudabaugh, Billy Wilson, Tom O'Folliard and Charles Bowdre, rode into Fort Sumner, where an ambush had been set up by Sheriff Garrett and his deputies. Tom O'Folliard was killed in the waylay. The Kid, who, at this point, had escaped arrest, was recaptured after Charlie Bowdre was killed in Stinking Springs, New Mexico. Bowdre was mistaken for the Kid when he innocently put on the Kid's hat to feed his horse on December 23, 1880. Pickett, Rudabaugh, Wilson and the Kid were captured and incarcerated in Fort Sumner before they were transported to Las Vegas, New Mexico, for trial. A mob arose in Las Vegas when locals demanded the outlaws be turned over to them for justice. Billy was reported to have commented, "If I only had my Winchester, I'd lick the whole crowd."

After a trip to Santa Fe to meet with the governor, Billy found out that he did not have a friend in the Governor's Palace and was sent to Mesilla, New Mexico, for trial in April 1881. During the trial, the Kid was found guilty of the murder of Sheriff Brady and was sentenced to hang on May 13, 1881. Billy was moved back to Lincoln to await his sentence. While he was incarcerated, Billy shot two jailers in his escape from the Lincoln County Courthouse, which housed the jail. Controversy still swirls over how he obtained the weapon he used to shoot Deputy Bell. Townspeople were said to have helped Billy, as they were partial to the boy outlaw. There was no doubt about the rifle the Kid used on Deputy Bob Olinger, since he used the lawman's own weapon to kill him.

While on the run, Billy returned to Fort Sumner on July 13, 1881. It was there that he met his fate by the hands of Sheriff Pat Garrett in the early morning hours of July 14, 1881. The outlaw had allegedly stopped at the home of Pete Maxwell to visit his rumored girlfriend, Paulita Maxwell, Pete's sister, when, as he unsuspectingly entered a dark room, he sensed something was not right. The twenty-one-year-old was shot in his stockinged feet, while he was armed with only a knife that he was using to cut some jerky from a cow carcass that was hanging in the kitchen. Billy went down in history as a romantically tragic character whom many did not want to see die. Controversy still surrounds the Kid's death; rumors that he survived and moved to Mexico made their rounds in New Mexico. Many farmers claimed they had dinner with the Kid as he made his way to Mexico after his supposed death, and others even claimed to be the Kid outright.

No matter your belief, Fort Sumner is the home of Billy the Kid's grave. The large concrete headstone is carved with the word "PALS" and includes not only Billy's name but those of his good friends Charles Bowdre and Tom O'Folliard as well. The grave is thought to be close to the area where Billy and his friends were laid to rest, but floods have displaced some of the graves and no one is certain of their resting places.

The Kid's bad luck seems to have followed him in death as well, since his headstone, which was not erected until 1931, has been stolen twice. The first theft took place in 1950, after which the stone was not found for twenty-six years; it was eventually found in a backyard in Granbury, Texas. The next theft of the stone took place in 1981, after which it was recovered in Huntington Beach, California. The stone, which is so widely recognizable today, was also tipped over in 2012 when someone reached into the gated enclosure and pushed it over. The headstone is now secured and fenced off to prevent any more incidents.

Left: Old Mesilla was the New Mexico jail that once held the famous outlaw Billy the Kid as he awaited hanging. It is now a gift and souvenir shop. *Courtesy of the author's collection.*

Below: Fort Sumner is the site of Billy the Kid's grave. The original peaked headstone has been stolen twice and needed to be secured against further theft. *Courtesy of the author's collection.*

Bosque Redondo and the Long Walk

One of the most heartbreaking events in American and New Mexico history ended at Fort Sumner. The Cherokee experienced the tragic Trail of Tears, and the Navajos (the *Diné*) and the Mescalero Apaches (the *N'de*) experienced the equally tragic Long Walk.

The Navajos had long stirred up trouble for the Spanish and Mexican governments in the northwest region of the New Mexico Territory and along the Arizona border when they ruled the area before 1846. The purpose of the tribe's raids was to steal from the settlers livestock, food and sometimes women and children for slaves. Settler slaves would be used within the tribal region or sold to other tribes for horses and firearms. The Spanish would return the favor by conducting their own raids to procure the same commodities, creating a vicious circle of hate.

A commander of the United States' forces, often described as aggressive, ruthless and brilliant, Colonel James H. Carleton of the California Column was sent in to deal with the "Indian menace." It was no secret that Carleton had a dislike of the Native people; he had seen the carnage caused by many of the tribes in New Mexico. He was described as being "one of the best

This image of Fort Sumner was discovered in the National Archives by an archivist who recognized the buildings. It had previously been mislabeled. *Courtesy of the Southeastern New Mexico Historical Society.*

of the old army and ante-bellum [*sic*] days" in Ralph Twitchell's *Leading Facts of New Mexican History*. Carleton and his company of First Dragoons were stationed at Fort Union from 1851 to 1852, and they assisted in the construction of the fort. Under the direction of Major General Edwin Vose Sumner, Carleton and his First Dragoons traveled to the eastern portion of the New Mexico Territory and visited the Bosque Redondo (Round Wood) site on many occasions. The Bosque Redondo was known to travelers. There are reports that Francisco Vázquez de Coronado stopped here in 1541 and that Antonio de Espejo followed him in 1583. The Comanche tribe was also familiar with the area. Carleton was impressed with the land, and when he returned in 1862 as a commander, he recommended to President Abraham Lincoln that a forty-square-mile Native reservation be built there—the recommendation was approved.

Today, the brick footprint of Fort Sumner is a reminder of the large military force that once lived on the site. *Courtesy of the author's collection.*

Due to the intense raids committed by the Mescalero Apaches in the Fort Stanton area, Carleton was forced to make war against the tribe, even though his Union soldiers were not completely prepared. Confederate troops held much of the settled regions of the New Mexico and Arizona Territories and had captured most of the Union supplies; there was not enough time before the Confederate's advanced to replenish the supplies needed for the upwards of nine thousand Union troops. Knowing his reputation, Colonel Carleton enlisted the help of Colonel Christopher "Kit" Carson and his five companies of the First New Mexico Volunteer Infantry from Fort Stanton. Carson, who had been in command of numerous forts in New Mexico, had a long and notorious career as a mountain man, trapper, wilderness guide, dime novel hero and Indian agent for the Ute and Jicarilla Apache tribes in Taos, New Mexico. Carson had also just seen action in the decisive Civil War battle in New Mexico, the Battle of Valverde, in April 1862.

Above: A group of Navajos line up in front of a Fort Sumner building to await rations. The Natives were unaware of how to use the food they were given. *Courtesy of the Southeastern New Mexico Historical Society.*

Right: Kit Carson had a reputation as an Indian fighter, but he was said to have been disillusioned with the army by the Fort Sumner experiment. *Courtesy of the Southeastern New Mexico Historical Society.*

Colonel Carleton's orders were to "slay the men without parleying, if they resisted, and to bring the women and children in as prisoners." This famous quote from Carleton is a chilling insight to the inner workings of his military mind:

> *All Indian men of that tribe are to be killed whenever and wherever you can find them. If the Indians send in a flag of truce, say to the bearer that you have been sent to punish them for their treachery and their crimes, that you have no power to make peace, that you are there to kill them wherever you can find them.*

There were no treaties offered and no terms were accepted except for total surrender to become prisoners of war. Carson spared no time in enacting Carleton's orders and killed two of the main chiefs of the Mescalero tribe in the first battle. Many warriors lost their lives during the battle; the women and children were captured as was ordered.

Most of the remaining tribal members either escaped east to live with the Comanches or moved south into Mexico. The remaining Mescalero chieftains and their Indian agent, Lorenzo Labadi, went to Santa Fe to plead with the government for peace. The small group was told that they must reside on a reservation if they wanted peace and that the government would help them become self-sufficient; this help included the provision of livestock, such as horses, sheep and cattle, that the tribe could use as food. The government also promised, should they refuse, the tribes would be "harassed by the soldiers until they were all killed or captured." This was the cruelest treaty the tribe was ever given; approximately five hundred of the tribe's members agreed to the terms.

After their surrender, the nomadic Mescalero Apaches, along with a few Jicarilla Apache chiefs, were dispatched from their home in the beautiful White Mountains near Ruidoso, Capitan and Lincoln, New Mexico, to the dry, flat, undeveloped Bosque Redondo, located along the highly alkaline Pecos River. Mescalero Apache chief Cadete thought the move to be a far better alternative to being eradicated by the United States military.

Once the tribal members arrived at Bosque Redondo, they quickly realized that development of the land was necessary to sustain the tribe through the winter. Carleton immediately put the five hundred Mescalero to work; the tribe was unaccustomed to the work of farmers and laborers, since they traditionally traveled and lived off the land on a seasonal basis.

In his book *Life Among the Apaches,* John Cremony wrote:

> *Five days after* [the Mescalero Apaches'] *arrival in camp, Mr. Labadi, the Indian Agent, came to me and said: "These Indians are in great destitution. They consumed their rations two days ago and have nothing to eat. There are many women and children among them; two more days must elapse before rations are again distributed. Their warriors have asked that they be allowed to go hunting. The plains close by are filled with antelope, which may easily be taken. I have been to Captain Updegraff, but he will not hear of the proposition; please try and see what you can do, for otherwise they may attempt to escape the reservation."*

Cremony later wrote that he spoke with Captain Updegraff and was granted permission to give the warriors forty-eight hours to hunt, but he also had to give written assurances that he and his men would accompany them. After the terms were given to the tribe the next morning, fifty-nine Native men and fifteen women, along with Cremony's men, began the hunt. This was the first of the many attempts for the Native tribe and the United States soldiers to work together to make the reservation inhabitable. The Mescalero Apaches had learned to farm and were doing well in their new environment—until the arrival of the Navajos.

The Navajos were causing a great deal of trouble in the northwestern New Mexico Territory by attacking wagon trains and Fort Defiance. They heard about the plight of the Apaches and had already experienced severe treatment by the United States government in 1846, so they asked for a peace treaty. General Carleton agreed to the treaty but warned the tribe that, should this treaty be broken, there would be swift and dire consequences; the United States government had offered seven treaties that were broken by the Navajos prior to 1863. Unfortunately, this treaty was broken in less than six weeks and war was declared on the Navajos by the United States. The elders of the tribe, who were referred to as the "Peace Party," explained that the fault of the broken treaty laid with the younger warriors of the tribe, who could not be controlled. Carleton told the Peace Party to separate from the more hostile members of the tribe and to go to Bosque Redondo, where he assured them that they would be taken care of. Carleton also assured them that a refusal to comply would end in war. Since none of the Navajos showed up to begin the journey to Fort Sumner on the given deadline of July 20, 1863, war was declared.

The Pecos River, which runs behind Fort Sumner, provided water for crops and drinking, although it has a high alkaline content. *Courtesy of the author's collection.*

FRONTIER FORTS AND OUTPOSTS OF NEW MEXICO

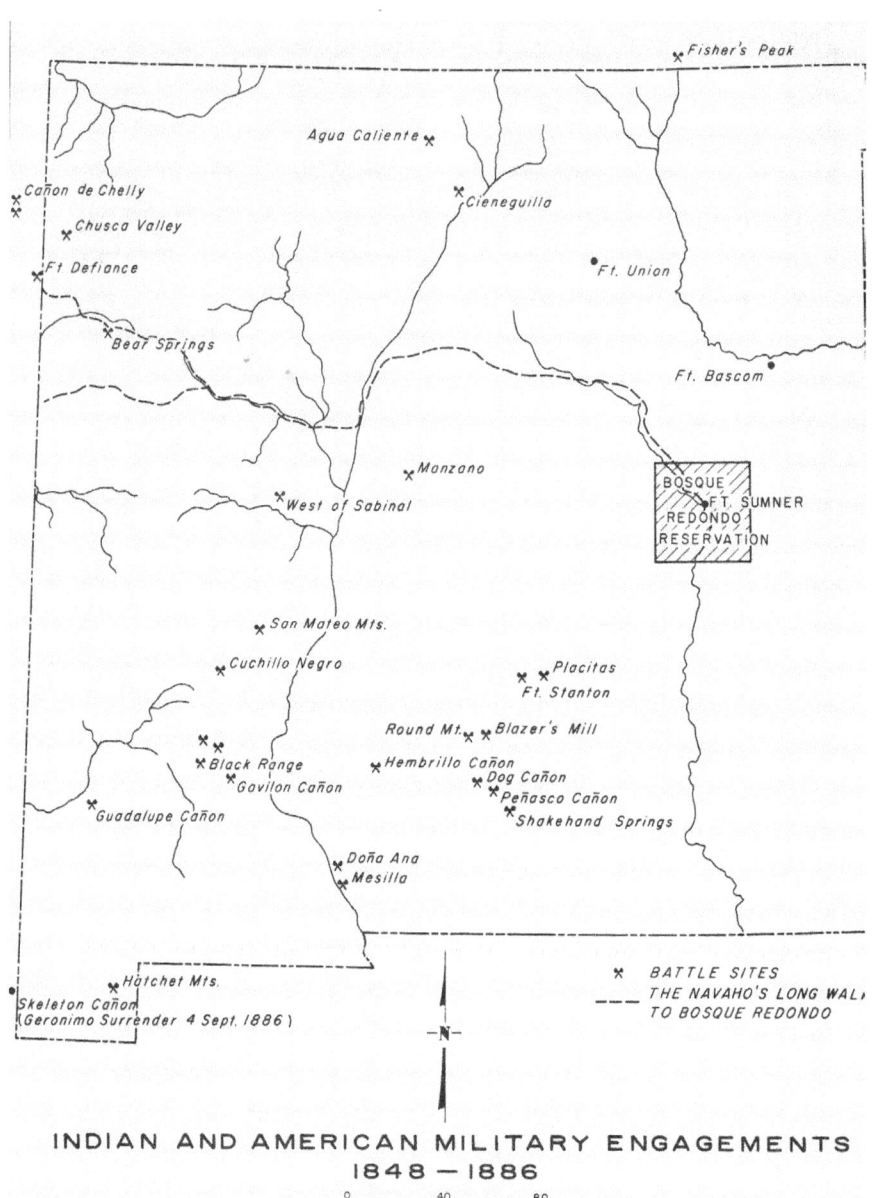

The New Mexico Territory has many Native American battle sites where the clash between cultures came to a head. *Courtesy of the author's collection.*

Once again, Colonel Carson and his New Mexico Volunteers were sent to wage war against the Navajos in a scorched-earth fashion. His orders were the same during this battle as they had been in the battle against the Mescaleros; Carson was ruthless and managed to kill 301 and wound 87 men, and he captured 703 women and children. Carson's campaign lasted until January 6, 1864, which gave the tribe no time to prepare. The Navajos' crops and *hogans* (homes) were burned, their water wells tainted and their livestock either killed or seized.

After the initial battle with the Navajos, 390 soldiers commanded by Carson left Fort Canby (a temporary fort located north of Fort Wingate) to once again engage with the Navajos on January 23, 1864. During this battle, more Natives were killed and 200 surrendered. Carson's plan was to treat the captives well, by giving them food and clothes and setting them free, so that they would tell other Natives that they would also be treated well if they surrendered. The plan worked—too well; the Navajos surrendered to Forts Canby and Wingate, as well as Los Pinos in southern Colorado, by the thousands (10,000 to be exact). Starvation was the main motivation for the surrender of two-thirds of the Navajo tribe.

Despite harsh winter conditions (snow has been known to be nearly four feet deep during the winter in the central plains of New Mexico), the Navajo captives were forced to march to Fort Sumner and Bosque Redondo, which were a torturous 450 miles away. Food and shelter were scarce along the four routes taken by the fifty different groups that made the trek to Bosque Redondo during the three-year timespan. According to Navajo oral histories, no care was given to their people during the Long Walk; should someone fall behind, they were either shot or left to die. The Navajo tribe would suffer a 20 percent loss of their tribal members (over two thousand people) before reaching their destination. Upon reaching Bosque Redondo, the Navajos learned that they would be forced to share the reservation with a sworn enemy—the Mescalero Apaches. The Navajo word for the Bosque Redondo was *H'weeldi*, which means "place of suffering."

Unable to calculate the exact number of Native people who would be residing on the reservation, the United States government far underestimated the overwhelming amounts of charges it had in its care (over nine thousand)—and more continued to trickle in every day. There was no housing available for the Navajos, and they were forced to reside in dirt pits covered loosely by hides or tree branches. Like the Mescalero Apaches, the Navajos were put to work directly; they helped build Fort Sumner, planted cottonwoods and dug a diversion dam and the *acequia*

Replicas of the twig huts that provided the only shelter the Navajos to escape the bitter cold at Fort Sumner after enduring a grueling five-hundred-mile walk. *Courtesy of the author's collection.*

madre (mother ditch). This noble tribe was basically reduced to slavery, as they were forced to dig a six-mile-long, ten-foot-wide and four-foot-deep water trench from the Pecos River to Fort Sumner for irrigation. The acequia madre is still in use today, although it is now much deeper.

Carleton had envisioned the reservation to be a utopia of sorts, where the tribes would work together and build a thriving self-sufficient farming community. Even Carleton's troops were secretly mocking the general's idealism by calling Bosque Redondo "Carletonia." It was termed a social experiment but soon proved to be a complete failure due to the inability of the soldiers to understand the structures of Native society. The U.S. government did not realize, or care at that time, that the two tribes they had placed together were enemies. They also did not care about the fact the Mescalero Apaches were nomadic and that the Navajos were traditionally a pastoral people or that neither tribe liked living in large communal groups.

The Mescaleros (nearly five hundred strong) were unable to endure captivity any longer and escaped in the middle of the night in February 1865. They felt betrayed; they had been told they would only be at Bosque Redondo a few months, and the farming they were forced to do there went against their beliefs, as they thought it did damage to Mother Earth. A few of the Mescaleros who could not travel quickly were left behind to tend campfires that they built in order to fool the soldiers into thinking the tribe was still on the site. The Mescaleros were not recaptured possibly because the soldiers were glad that there were five hundred fewer mouths to feed. Today, the Mescalero Apache tribe resides on the 400,000-acre Mescalero Apache Reservation, which includes some of the most breathtaking landscapes in south central New Mexico. The tribe is extremely prosperous, with casino operations at the spectacular Inn of the Mountain Gods and the ski resort Ski Apache, which boasts, at a height of 8,900 feet, one of the longest zip lines in the world.

It would be three long years before the Navajos would regain their freedom. When reports of the deplorable conditions at the reservation reached Washington, D.C., General William T. Sherman was sent to meet with the thirty Navajo chiefs at Bosque Redondo who relayed the stories of their confinement. From this meeting, the Treaty of 1868 was established and signed, and it stated that the Navajo tribe, which was now known as the Navajo Nation, was free to return to their lands and be given rations for ten years, breeding stock and reservations; however, they were also told that they were to send their children to government-sponsored schools. It

Behind Fort Sumner is the six-mile-long acequia madre (mother ditch), which was dug by Navajo men. It is still in use today. *Courtesy of the author's collection.*

is thought that the main motivation behind the schools was the quick and cheap integration of Natives into Anglo-American society. Native children were taken from their homes, forced to wear clothes that were foreign to them and told to cut their hair in order to conform to what was deemed "normal," as the tribe was still seen as a threat to the New Mexico and Arizona Territories. The Treaty of 1868 also stipulated that the Navajos were to "make no opposition to the military posts or roads now established, or that may be established." The Bosque Redondo Memorial contains one of three known copies of the Treaty of 1868, which is kept in a locked vault and can be revealed to visitors by a memorial staff member.

The long journey home was far different from the Long Walk; the children and elderly were transported in wagons; others rode horseback and a few walked. This time, there were no threats of being shot for lagging behind.

Today, the Navajo Nation covers over 17 million acres of northwestern New Mexico, northeastern Arizona and southeastern Utah, making it the largest reservation in the United States. The Navajo Nation is also the largest Native American tribe in the United States.

Fort Sumner Today

Known today as the gravesite of the infamous outlaw Billy the Kid, Fort Sumner also had a sad and tragic purpose during the Long Walk, which landed it in the history books in a less than bright light. The tiny town by the same name in the far reaches of east central New Mexico, near the Texas border, embraces its notoriety through its excellent museums, which celebrate Billy the Kid's life and death and mourn the events at Bosque Redondo.

In the town, visitors can find the beautiful Bosque Redondo Memorial, which shares the tragic story of the land on which it is built. The Bosque Redondo Memorial is on scarred land, which saw great tragedy and heartache; it is a beautiful, yet humbling, tribute to the two Native tribes that endured unimaginable horrors. Both the Bosque Redondo Memorial and Fort Sumner are New Mexico State Monuments. As visitors walk the grounds of Fort Sumner they feel a reverence, a quiet solitude, which is a far cry from the experience of the Native tribes that were encamped there from 1863 to 1868.

Today, to embrace the celebrity of the boy outlaw Billy the Kid, Fort Sumner throws Old Fort Days in the second week of June. The celebration includes a tombstone race, a parade and a fiddler's contest, among other festivities. Watersports are also available on the Pecos River, Sumner Lake State Park

Bosque Redondo Memorial, opened in June 2005, was designed by Navajo architect David Sloan to resemble a Navajo hogan and a Mescalero Apache teepee. *Courtesy of the author's collection.*

(which is sixteen miles northeast of Fort Sumner) and the Bosque Redondo Lake (which is located five miles southeast of town). The small village is located exactly halfway between Albuquerque, New Mexico and Lubbock, Texas.

Directions and Information

To reach Fort Sumner, drive 6.5 miles southeast of the village of Fort Sumner. Then, drive 3.0 miles east on Highway 60/84 and 3.5 miles south on Billy the Kid Drive.

Fort Sumner
3647 Billy the Kid Drive
Fort Sumner, NM 88119

To plan your visit, call the Bosque Redondo Memorial Center at (575) 355-2573 for more information.

Hours:
It is recommended that you call ahead in case of closures.
The fort is open from 8:30 a.m. to 4:30 p.m., Wednesday through Monday (it is closed on Tuesday).
The fort is closed on Thanksgiving, Christmas, New Year's Day and Easter. Admission is free for children sixteen years old and under. Admission is also free to New Mexico residents on Sunday and New Mexico seniors on Wednesday.

FORT UNION (1851–1891)

Fort Union was established in 1851 at the crossroads of two westward trails called the Mountain and the Cimarron. Soon, it became the largest military fort in the region, and during the nineteenth century, it became known as a fort for young America, as it protected the thousands of wagons full of settlers that traversed the Santa Fe Trail. The heavy wagons cut deep ruts into the earth, and remnants of the trail can still be seen today.

Small adobe structures and partial walls are all that remain of the third Fort Union, which is now protected as a National Monument. Wind-swept,

LONGEST INHABITED NEW MEXICO FORTS

Deep ruts of the Santa Fe Trail, cut by the wagon wheels of thousands of travelers, can still be seen outside of Fort Union. *Courtesy of the author's collection.*

The supply depot of Fort Union was once a bustling spot where travelers and politicians gathered on their way to Santa Fe. *Courtesy of the author's collection.*

grassy plains stretch for miles around the fort in three directions, which once gave it the advantage of long sight lines. Unlike other frontier forts built during the same time period, there are no close mountains that could provide ample opportunity for an ambush surrounding the Fort Union. Visitors are very likely to see pronghorns and other wild creatures during the eight-mile drive from Interstate 25 to the monument site, but one can only imagine what the ride to the fort must have been like aboard a covered wagon.

During its forty years of existence, Fort Union was known as not only the largest fort in the territory but also the most important, as it played a crucial role during the Civil War at Glorieta Pass. Since its location was in the heart of Native country, the fort was also a vital supply depot for those traveling west and locals.

First Fort Union (1851–1861)

Hastily built in 1851 by the soldiers themselves, the first Fort Union consisted of rough-hewn timber and adobe shacks that were barely habitable. It was quite evident that the soldiers were not construction workers and that they had no clue how to build a fort. The first officers and their families had to resort to living in canvas tents until these buildings were complete, but they were heard to say that the tents provided better shelter. This fort included a supply depot, a hospital, a mechanics corral and a fine bakery.

The first fort was successful in protecting the profitable trade route from the protests and attacks from the Jicarilla Apaches and Utes, who were not happy to see the western expansion of the white man. Soldiers from Fort Union engaged with the Native tribes on many occasions while protecting white travelers in the region.

By 1856, the original fort, made of timber from the Turkey Mountains, was falling into complete disrepair and needed to be abandoned, but it remained in service until 1861. At that time, the construction of the second Fort Union began, as did the Civil War.

Second Fort Union (1861–1862)

The second Fort Union was often called the "Star Fort" due to its star-shaped earthen fieldwork that provided a safe entrenchment for the camp and bombproofing for the magazine and storehouse. This fort would

Longest Inhabited New Mexico Forts

The second Fort Union was once referred to as the "Star Fort" due to the star-shaped construction. These formations can still be seen. *Courtesy of the Library of Congress.*

be located one mile east of the original fort and would later become Fort Union's arsenal. For protection, the fort was fitted with twenty-eight cannon platforms and a central magazine. It was the duty of arsenal workers to ensure that all firearms, large and small, and ammunition were in working order. When new firearms arrived at the fort, they had to be field tested to make sure the soldiers would be able to operate them quickly and efficiently.

It was during the time of the second Fort Union that Confederate eyes began to look greedily at the depot. Henry H. Sibley helped construct the arsenal, so he was well-aware of the storage capabilities it provided. When he resigned his commission with the Union in order to become a Confederate officer, he had every intention of capturing Fort Union for the Confederacy. With a win at the Battle of Valverde, Sibley was poised to complete his plan with extra confidence. This made Fort Union vitally important to ensuring a Union victory in the Battle of Glorieta Pass.

Battle of Glorieta Pass

Confederate forces from Texas marched under the command of Brigadier General Henry H. Sibley and flew the large red flag emblazoned with a single white star—Sibley's flag. During the campaign push forward to Santa Fe, the Confederates had seen several victories: they had occupied the town of Mesilla, captured an entire Union force under the command of Major Isaac Lynde at St. Augustine Springs, defeated a second, superior Union force at the Battle of Valverde, occupied Albuquerque and raised the Confederate flag in the plaza of the capital city of Santa Fe on March 23, 1862. The Confederacy also enjoyed a surge of recruitments in the West, especially in southern New Mexico, Utah and Colorado (which was due to morale issues within the Union forces).

It was widely rumored that the New Mexico Territory had a treasure trove of arsenals, holding around eight thousand rifles and thirty cannons for the war effort, that were prime for the taking. Following the Battle of Valverde, Sibley knew his troops needed the weapons and supplies that were stored at Fort Union in order for their journey to the rich gold fields of Colorado and California to be a complete success. The Rebels were working to spread slavery into the western territories and, eventually, as far south as Mexico. Fresh off their recent victories, Sibley's Confederate troops were confident in their plan to capture the largest fort in the region.

When Lieutenant Colonel Edward R.S. Canby got wind of the Confederates' plan, he immediately requested that the governor of Colorado send reinforcements. The request was answered by the First Regiment of Colorado Volunteers, which consisted of ten companies of men. When the men arrived at Fort Union, thirteen days after they were requested, they were

Left: Sundials were an important part of keeping nineteenth-century military operations on time. This sundial is still in use, although the gnomon (the part of a sundial that casts a shadow) has been replaced. *Courtesy of the Library of Congress.*

Below: A vintage image of Fort Union Officer's Row, where workers had once begun to tear down the fort before preservation efforts began. *Courtesy of the Library of Congress.*

exhausted from their four-hundred-mile march. The appearance of the 950 Colorado Volunteers raised the spirits and hopes of the 800 troops that were already stationed at Fort Union. Under the command of Colonel John P. Slough, 1,342 men left the safety of Fort Union on March 22 to intercept the Confederate forces at Glorieta Pass. Confident in their commands, neither Canby nor Sibley took to the battlefield with their troops. Canby remained at Fort Craig, and it was rumored that Sibley had celebrated a bit too strongly and remained in Albuquerque with an aggravated liver disorder.

Unaware of the Colorado reinforcements, the Confederates, under orders from Sibley, continued their march with the Second Texas Mounted Rifles (under the command of Major Charles L. Pyron) and the Fifth Texas Mounted Rifles (under the command of Major John S. Schropshire) toward Fort Union. Colonel William Scurry, along with the Fourth Texas Regiment, First Battalion and Seventh Texas Mounted Volunteers, headed to Galisteo to meet up with Pyron on the Glorieta Pass. The pass was a strategic location on the Santa Fe Trail and gaining control of it would ensure the Confederates' military superiority over the Union troops.

Pyron camped at Johnson's Ranch in Apache Canyon on March 25. The ranch was later claimed by Pyron as his Confederate headquarters. Union commander Major John Chivington and four hundred infantrymen were planning on surprising a small group of Rebels, but they soon learned that the Confederates' numbers were larger than they originally thought. Chivington camped at Kozlowski's Ranch, where he was able to capture Confederate scouts in the area. Armed with the information gleaned from the scouts, one being a Union deserter, Chivington and his men were able to plan their attack

The two forces surprised each other in Apache Canyon, and Pyron opened fire on the Union troops with two howitzers. Chivington deployed two companies to go behind the Rebels and force them back by placing batteries on the surrounding bluffs. Chivington's plan soon worked, and the Texans were forced to back down the canyon.

Company F of the First Colorado Volunteers, under the direction of Captain Samuel H. Cook, charged the Confederate forces three times. They completed their first charge by leaping a creek with 103 horses, and the other two were direct charges. These charges ultimately forced the Texans up a side canyon, where they were captured. Since both sides had dead and wounded men to care for, Chivington agreed to a truce until 8:00 a.m. on March 27. This gave each side a chance to bury their dead and treat the wounded. Chivington commissioned Pigeon's Ranch as a field hospital,

The mountain howitzer was one of the most feared weapons used in the West. *Courtesy of the author's collection.*

and he sent the Confederate prisoners to Fort Union under a heavily armed guard. During the truce, each side was reinforced with new troops and supply wagons. The Confederates left their supply wagons at Johnson's Ranch, because they thought they would only slow troop movement.

On March 28, 1862, after a day of rest and regrouping, the Battle at Glorieta Pass, which has recently been referred to as the "Gettysburg of the West," was fought in New Mexico. With information of the highly reinforced Confederate force, Major Chivington decided to take 430 men and circle around behind the Confederate troops while the other Union forces were moving against them directly. Confederate Colonel Scurry lobbed artillery at the Union troops, which forced them to fight from behind the trees and rocks and left their cavalry units dismounted. The Texans advanced and fired their artillery for three hours, which disabled two of their howitzers.

This is all that remains of the Fort Union Depot officer's quarters. Preservation is an ongoing battle for the fort staff. *Courtesy of the author's collection.*

They also gained control of Sharpshooter's Ridge, giving them a clear shot on the Union artillery. In order to obtain the Union's supply wagons, the Texan's surged forward one last time but were pushed back.

By 5:00 p.m., Colonel Slough called his Union forces back to regroup. This was not a popular decision, but he stated that they had received a new command to "reconnoiter and harass the enemy." The Texans took Slough's actions as a surrender, and they were thrilled to have won another battle against the Federal troops. However, their good thoughts soon turned to those of lamenting when they received news that the Confederate supply wagon had been destroyed. The First New Mexico Volunteers, commanded by Lieutenant Manuel Chavez, were able to traverse the Glorieta Mesa, which gave them a wonderful view of Johnson's Ranch one thousand feet below. Using ropes, the First New Mexico Volunteers were able to climb down the mountain to surprise the Confederate troops who had been left to guard the supplies. The wagons, which were said to have contained enough supplies for a small army, were demolished and the animals were bayoneted, leaving the Confederate invasion in a world of hurt. Devastated by the news, Colonel Scurry sent Slough a flag of truce and requested two days of cease fire, which were granted. This Union maneuver had dealt "a death blow to the hopes of the Confederacy," according to his report. Once again, the dead were buried and the wounded treated, but after two days at Johnson's Ranch without supplies, the Texans were forced to retreat to Santa Fe. Sibley requested more supplies from the governor of Texas but received no reply. Union losses during the Battle of Glorieta Pass totaled 150 men, and the Confederate forces lost 300 troops.

Two other small skirmishes occurred during the Confederate retreat. The first was the Battle of Albuquerque, which was fought on April 10, 1862. During the battle, Sibley and Canby exchanged cannon shots until residents of Old Town in Albuquerque complained about the noise and being in danger. This was the only battle fought within Albuquerque city limits, and it is believed that the Confederates buried their cannons and howitzers there when they left under the cover of darkness.

The second skirmish took place on April 18, 1862, near what is now known as the Bosque Farm Project near modern-day Los Lunas. During the Battle of Peralta in Bosque Farms, the Confederate army took over the home of Governor Henry Connelly, causing over $30,000 worth of damage. All but seven days' worth of the Confederates' rations were destroyed. These rations were saved in order to get the Rebel forces across the Rio Grande and back to Texas. As it happens, during the spring in New Mexico, the runoff from the snow on the mountains causes the river to swell, and this swelling forced the Confederates to leave sixty wagons on the riverbank. The nearly three thousand Confederate men climbed through the mountains to avoid Fort Craig on their journey back to Texas. The New Mexico Territory was under Union control for the remainder of the Civil War.

Third Fort Union (1863–1891)

When visitors walk around the fort site today, they are able to see the crumbling remains of the third Fort Union, which was built with the help of civilians and the Confederate prisoners taken during the Battle of Glorieta Pass. This fort was the best constructed and the most permanent of the structures that were built on the site.

The jail at Fort Union also shared space with the laundress's quarters. It is one of the best-preserved buildings on the site. *Courtesy of the author's collection.*

As the largest fort in New Mexico, Fort Union included a quartermaster depot, which was a central supply hub along the Santa Fe Trail and saw upward of one hundred wagon trains, which could contain up to two hundred wagons in each, pass through daily. The sheer number of migrants that headed west was staggering—they all wanted to get rich in the gold fields of California. It is also from this depot that thousands of tons of supplies were shipped out to the forty-six regional posts that supported the military system in the New Mexico Territory.

If the saying "There's safety in numbers" is true, Fort Union lived up to it by being one of the safest forts in the territory. Officers would bring their families to live at the fort, which provided a great amount of entertainment and education for their children. The wives of the officers and enlisted men would also coordinate social events, but at times, the soldiers would become bored with the mundane life at the fort and seek other forms of entertainment.

Loma Parda

Seven miles from Fort Union, there was a small agricultural town by the name of Loma Parda. In its early days, Loma Parda was a quiet farming community, but when the fort was constructed nearby, opportunity seekers saw the town as a gold mine. Julian Baca opened a dance hall, casino and cantina that featured gambling and cribs in the back, where prostitutes could entertain their clients.

Drunkenness had always been a problem at the military forts, where the days were long and tedious, and communities like Loma Parda provided the soldiers with an outlet. Euphemistically known as "hog ranches," the lure of women and whiskey from towns like these was too much for some of the soldiers. Fort Union had a huge problem with its soldiers being absent without leave (AWOL) after a night out in Loma Parda, sometimes to the tune of fifteen or twenty a day. Many of these men would try to sneak their nightly denizens onto the fort as laundresses and beg their commanders to allow the women to follow them on marches—usually to no avail.

The prostitution ring, which mainly consisted of ladies from Santa Fe, predated the third Fort Union. Some of these women had set up shop in the nearby caves in 1852, trading their feminine wiles for food and supplies. The fort's warehouses lost 9,379 pounds of bacon, 5,254 pounds of sugar, 4,303 pounds of coffee, as well as candles, soap and dried peaches to this trade within a six-month span of time. It was also determined that 90 percent of the cases of venereal disease and smallpox at the fort originated from these women.

Captain Sykes of Fort Union set out to stop the thievery and debauchery by luring the two main women of the trade, Maria Delores Trujigue y Rivale and Maria Alvina Chaireses (who was also known as Black Sus), into the fort for a visit. When they complied, they were immediately arrested and placed in the stockades, where their heads were shaved; thus, the caves were called "Bald Woman Caves" from that time forward.

Over the years, visitations to Loma Parda by the soldiers were prohibited, but the den of iniquity proved to be a stronger draw than punishment at the fort. Many soldiers would lose their entire paychecks, sixteen dollars per month, in one night. Loma Parda would outlast the fort and continue operations well into World War I.

Indian Wars

Because of its central location in the heart of Indian country, Fort Union was often called on to lend support to settlers and townsfolk in skirmishes and wars against the Native tribes. While Kit Carson and his First New Mexico Volunteers were sparing with the Navajos and Mescalero Apaches in the Northwest and Central New Mexico Territory, Fort Union's engineers began working on the reservations that were to hold these tribes at Bosque Redondo and Fort Sumner. Some of the Navajos who were walking to Fort Sumner from the Ojo Caliente reservation and other parts of the northern territory passed through Fort Union during the Long Walk.

Supplies and the Fort Union Regulars, who replaced the First New Mexico Volunteers after the Civil War, were provided to lend support to General Philip Sheridan's 1868 and 1869 campaign against the Cheyenne, Sioux, Arapahoe, Kiowa and Comanche tribes. Troops from Fort Union were also sent to fight in the Red River War in Texas from 1874 to 1875 against the Comanche, Kiowa, Arapaho and Cheyenne tribes. The war was fought in order to forcibly move the Natives from the Southern Plains to different reservations in Indian Territory (modern-day Oklahoma). This war was fought against a number of famous Native leaders, including the famed Quanah Parker, and it came to be known as the Second Battle of Adobe Walls. The United States Army was victorious in this war. The first Ninth Cavalry unit, otherwise known as the Buffalo Soldiers, was sent to Fort Union in 1875 to help with the Indian Wars as well. These campaigns proved to be the final battles in the Indian Wars for Fort Union.

One of the most majestic ruins is that of Officer's Row. The once stately rooms have been reduced to mere skeletons of their former selves. *Courtesy of the author's collection.*

Demise of Fort Union

With the arrival of the Santa Fe Railway in 1879, the usefulness of Fort Union as a supply depot began to wane, and it eventually closed its arsenal in 1882. In 1891, Fort Union was ordered to close, and all of its troops, as well as its prisoners, were sent to Fort Wingate in the northwestern region of the New Mexico Territory. The hospital closed on April 20, 1891, and the last soldier left his post at Fort Union on May 15, 1891. The once mighty fort was left to languish in the harsh elements, and Mother Nature did her best to reclaim the dirt from the adobe bricks.

Fort Union National Monument was established on June 28, 1954, in order to protect and preserve this amazing site for future generations. It is because of this action that visitors are still able to explore Fort Union today.

Fort Union Today

As visitors drive up New Mexico 161, they can see the remnants of the Fort Union Arsenal (the first Fort Union) that was so prized by the Confederate forces. Today, Fort Union also boasts a wonderful museum and gift shop. Visitors are encouraged to take a self-guided tour of the fort ruins and many displays along its paths. As the bugle sounds over the public address system, visitors should stop and take a moment to imagine what life was like in the turbulent, early days of New Mexico, when every day brought new threats of danger.

The peace that envelops Fort Union today was hard-earned and is almost deceiving; all that can be heard are the kestrels and grasshoppers calling to each other. Visitors should keep a sharp eye out for the ground squirrels and lizards that also call this open plain their home, and when the warm weather hits, they should be on high alert for possible rattlesnakes. Should a visitor see a rattlesnake, the park suggests that they back away slowly, go around it and report it to a park ranger.

Hats, sunglasses and water are suggested for walking tours.

Fort Union hosts many events to introduce the public, especially children, to the fascinating history of the fort. Fort Union Days are held in June and feature many presentations and hands-on events.

Gone are the days when Fort Union was a congested hub of activity, when the thousands of wagons heading west would cut deep ruts in the ground and when America was young, but we can keep that time alive by supporting historic preservation efforts.

A United States Army supply wagon sits proudly in front of the ruins of Officer's Row at Fort Union. *Courtesy of the author's collection.*

Directions and Information

To reach Fort Union, follow Interstate 25 North to exit 366 at Watrous, New Mexico, which is 28 miles north of Las Vegas, New Mexico. Follow New Mexico 161 for eight miles to Fort Union National Monument.

Fort Union National Monument
P. O. Box 127
Watrous, NM 87753

For more information, please call Fort Union Visitor Center at (505) 425-8025.

Hours:
During the summer (Memorial Day through Labor Day) the fort is open from 8:00 a.m. to 5:00 p.m.
During the winter (depending on weather) the fort is open from 8:00 a.m. to 4:00 p.m.
The park is closed on Thanksgiving, Christmas and New Year's Day.
Admission to the park is free. Picnic tables and drinking water and restrooms are available.

Fort Wingate (1862–1925)

Gallup, New Mexico, in McKinley County, plays host to Fort Wingate. This fort has had many locations and many names, so its history can get a bit confusing at times. First established as a military post in 1849 in Seboyeta, New Mexico, Fort Wingate's main purpose was to protect the town's citizens from the Navajos. The fort was moved to the town of Ojo del Gallo (Chicken Springs) in 1850 before being moved again near the town of San Rafael. It was at this location that the fort would come to be known as Camp Hay in the 1850s, but the name changes did not stop here.

A temporary post was established in 1860 at Shush B' Toh, Bear Springs (also known as Ojo de Oso by the Hispanic population) under the name of Fort Fauntleroy by Captain William Carpenter. The post was named for Colonel Thomas T. Fauntleroy of the First U.S. Dragoons. Amid a scandal, Colonel Fauntleroy resigned his Federal commission at the beginning of the Civil War and joined the Confederate movement. The fort was quickly renamed Fort Lyon in 1861 after General Nathaniel Lyon, who was killed in 1861 at the Battle of Wilson's Creek. This iteration of the fort was located on the road that is now known as Route 66, or Interstate 40, 140 miles west of Albuquerque as you travel to Fort Defiance, which is now in Arizona. It was placed under the command of Fauntleroy, who was sometimes known as Little Lord. He had fought the Natives of the West on and off for ten years before the Civil War.

Fauntleroy wrote a letter to General Winfield Scott in which he stated:

> *The greatest embarrassment arises from the fact that many of the claims set up against the Indians of New Mexico for plundering, stealing stock and*

the like, are either fabricated or to the considerable degree exaggerated, and if it was to be commenced up the simple presentation of these claims, the cause for war interminable, or the Indians must be extirpated.

Fauntleroy soon resigned his commission with the Union army and join the Confederates.

Fort Wingate I

Once again, the fort was renamed in 1862; this time, it was called Fort Wingate in honor of Captain Benjamin Wingate of the Fifth U.S. Infantry, who received wounds to his legs in the bloody Battle of Valverde. Although the garrison was withdrawn from Fort Lyon, a small mail station remained until General Edward Canby ordered a new fort to be established at the headwaters of the Gallo River in order to gain control over the Navajos, who had continually attacked settlers and Fort Defiance.

During the 1840s and 1850s, the United States was warring with Mexico over boundary disputes while also trying to squelch numerous uprisings from the Native tribes, who were attacking Mexican settlers in what would become the Arizona and New Mexico Territories. It was General Stephen Watts Kearny's mission to wage war in support of Westward Expansion. In 1846, Kearny proclaimed that he would be the protector of the New Mexico population, especially those who were being persecuted by the Navajos in the western part of the territory—thus, he created the need for Fort Wingate.

When Colonel Alexander W. Doniphan met with the Navajo leaders as a representative of Kearny, it was at Shush B'Toh, or Bear Springs, where Fort Fauntleroy was first located and Wingate would ultimately be built. During this meeting, a treaty was signed between Doniphan and fourteen Navajo leaders, and it stated that the Navajo, who call themselves the *Diné*, would cease their hostilities toward the American settlers, travelers and New Mexico residents and that all cattle and captives would be released. It was hoped that this treaty would lead to a better relationship between the Mexicans and the Navajos, but it did not last; the Navajos were not trusting of the people who had invaded the *Diné* homeland.

The original plan for Fort Wingate's layout was for it to be shaped like a circle within a square—the living quarters were to be in the square and the interior circle would contain storehouses, stables and shops. This design was quickly nixed, however, since it left no room for enlargement. Instead, a typical, rectangular design was adopted. Constructed mainly of adobe and sandstone, the buildings were simple, with window sashes and doorways trimmed in local lumber. Fort Wingate slowly melted away with every rainstorm, and the fact it was built on marshy ground did not help with its preservation. After multiple complaints written by the soldiers and commanders of the original Fort Wingate, General Carleton sent out an inspector from Washington, who concluded that their accounts were correct.

Kit Carson and four companies of the First New Mexico Volunteers (comprising mainly Hispanic men), who were also known as the First New Mexico Infantry Regiment, were ordered to garrison the fort by General Canby in 1864, just two years after his participation in the Battle of Valverde. Carson's orders were to round up and subdue the Navajos in the region.

Carson's campaign was against not only the Navajos but also the Comanches, Kiowas and Mescalero Apaches, which resulted in the deaths of hundreds of tribe members. The Navajos, who were residing close to Fort Wingate, were hit hardest, as Carson and his men ravaged their crops, burned their houses and slaughtered most of their animals. The Navajos' way of life was taken from them, so they surrendered to Fort Defiance and Fort Wingate. They surrendered in such great numbers that the forts were overwhelmed and did not know what to do with the Natives.

General James Carleton was well known for his distaste of Native people; he called the Navajos a "great evil" who "must be whipped and fear us before they will cease killing and robbing the people." The general's attitude and hatred came from his experiences in the Southwest, where he saw the results of Native attacks firsthand and was detailed to bury 34 victims of the Mountain Meadows Massacre just a day after he had buried 39. He also wrote a report that detailed an attack in which 120 men, women and children were killed on a wagon train—most of the victims were suspected to have been killed by the Paiutes in Utah. By the time he and the California Column arrived in New Mexico, Carleton's view of the Native tribes had become completely jaded.

The first Fort Wingate was used as a staging point for the Navajos, who were to participate in the Long Walk to Bosque Redondo at Fort Sumner, New Mexico. A Navajo elder spoke of the Long Walk in this way:

> *By slow stages, we traveled eastward by present Gallup and Chusbbito, Bear Spring, which is now called Fort Wingate. You ask how they treated us? If there was room, the soldiers put the women and children on the*

wagons. Some even let them ride behind them on their horses. I have never been able to understand a people who killed you one day and on the next played with your children.

The Navajos and the Long Walk were also described by author Ellen Threinen. She said, "The Long Walk and the roundup were culturally devastating to the Navajos, because they were transformed overnight from the strongest, richest group in the Southwest, to a straggling, starving band."

Navajo leaders Barboncito and Manuelito, finally tired of the troops burning their land, crops and houses, conceded to go with their tribes to Bosque Redondo at Fort Sumner, which was anywhere between four hundred and five hundred miles away from the Navajos' homelands. When word spread that these two leaders had surrendered, the rest of the Navajos began to make the trek to Fort Wingate and start the Long Walk. Although there were upward of fifty civilians working to build the fort, construction all but ceased as the flood of Navajos descended on the region.

Barboncito was known to have said about himself, if others asked about how he wanted to be remembered:

> *He would not go so far from his country but would remain with his family somewhere in the neighborhood of this Post* [Fort Wingate] *and that he did not intend to fight even if he were to be attacked by the troops—they might kill him but he would not run.*

In due course, Barboncito's resolve was worn away, and he gave in to the demands of the United States military.

Like at many of the remote forts in the New Mexico Territory, soldiers at Fort Wingate faced harsh conditions. Often, there was not enough food to go around, so many of them starved. Their shelters were barely able to keep out the elements, disease spread quickly through the ranks and, in 1878, the United States government did not pay troops for the entire year. Desperation and desertion became commonplace.

Fort Wingate II

In 1868, Fort Wingate II was established to replace Fort Wingate I. The garrison at Fort Wingate I was transferred to Fort Wingate II's location sixty miles away due to its decommission. Also, in 1868, the Navajo Nation returned to its reservation after the failed experiment at Fort Sumner. Fort Wingate was a resting spot for the caravans of people traveling the great distance, as it was the only fort located on Navajo land at the time.

General Douglas MacArthur called Fort Wingate home as a child between the years 1881 and 1882, when his father, Arthur MacArthur, was the captain in command of Company K, Thirteenth U.S. Infantry. The family was eventually transferred farther south to Fort Selden. Another famous military figure, "Black Jack" Pershing, also served as a lieutenant at Fort Wingate from 1889 to 1890. Pershing wrote to a friend about the condition of the first Fort Wingate saying, "This post is, no question, tumbled down, old quarters, though Stots is repairing it as fast as he can. The winters are severe, it is always bleak, and the surrounding country is barren absolutely."

The fewer than two hundred troops stationed at Fort Wingate settled disputes between the settlers, who were sometimes called secessionists due to their sympathetic feelings toward the Confederate cause, and the Navajos—mainly over the ownership of livestock—between 1868 and 1895. In 1891, Fort Wingate's garrison also helped the territory of Arizona deal with the increasing anger of the Hopi tribe, who fought to keep their children from being taken away and put in Indian boarding schools.

The Navajos were instrumental during the campaign against Apache leaders Victorio and Geronimo. Up to 400 Navajos served as scouts for the United States Army. The tribal members who joined were mostly free roaming and were told that if they did not want to be scouts, they would have to move to the reservations. The scouts were given six-month enlistments at Fort Wingate, and it is said that over 125 Navajos, or their families, received pensions from the government between the 1920s and 1940s.

Military reports show Fort Wingate II as consisting of "four rectangular C-plan structures," which were the company quarters. These quarters had a wash house and sink located behind each of the buildings. On the other side of the parade grounds sat the officer's quarters and the company storehouse. On July 2, 1896, Fort Wingate II was partially destroyed by a fire, but the subsistence storehouse was spared in this rampage.

By 1907, the Indian Wars, as they were known, began to taper off as Native leaders were either captured or killed. One last campaign occurred when two members of the Fifth Cavalry, originating from Fort Wingate, conducted a pursuit of an armed Navajo to the Four Corners area. This was the last armed expedition against the Navajos by the United States government—it resulted in one Navajo death.

The officer's quarter houses at Fort Wingate were some of the finest homes constructed at a New Mexico fort. *Courtesy of the Library of Congress.*

In 1914, Fort Wingate was used as a refuge for two thousand Mexican soldiers and their families, who were fleeing the bandit Pancho Villa during the Mexican Civil War. This occurred just two years after New Mexico became a state on January 6, 1912, and by 1918, the government had changed its focus from the Native tribes to World War I.

The fort's long military history of protecting the western part of the United States soon shifted to it becoming a storage depot for ammunition and ordnance, which lasted from 1940 to 1993. At the height of World War II in 1944, the government sights turned to nuclear power in order to stop the invading forces of Japan and Germany. The Manhattan Project was born to develop an atom bomb large enough to dissuade any superpowers from considering an invasion of United States soil. Fort Wingate supplied over one hundred tons of Composition B high explosives to the Manhattan Project to be used for the first Trinity test conducted near White Sands Missile Range. This made Fort Wingate the site with the largest store of high explosives in the world at this time with a reported eight hundred storage bunkers on site.

Navajo Code Talkers

During World War II, the Japanese forces were famous for being able to crack the intricate codes written by the United States government, so the government began to use Native languages for code instead. Code talking was already implemented in World War I with the Choctaws and Cherokees, for which they received no recognition, but with the recruitment of around five hundred Navajos to the marines during World War II, the Navajo language, called *Dinè bizaad*, became the official code language of the United States. As code, the Navajo language was complex, and code talkers were able to translate it into English in mere seconds. Some believe the Navajo language originates from the Tibetan and Chinese languages, which were brought to the New World over a land bridge. Whatever its origin, it proved to be baffling to the Japanese.

Without the amazing skills of the Navajo Code Talkers, who had to memorize an entire codebook of messages, World War II could have gone in a whole different direction, and we may have lost the Battle of Iwo Jima, during which they sent out over eight hundred messages alone. The Navajo Code Talkers worked nonstop relaying and translating over eight hundred messages by radio over two days without a single error. Unfortunately, we have lost a huge amount of these brave men to whom America owes a great debt of gratitude.

Fort Wingate was the proud home to these men, who changed the world with their native tongue. Ironically, one of the Navajo Code Talkers mused, "When I was going to boarding school [before the war], the U.S. government told us not to speak Navajo, but during the war, they wanted us to speak it!" Many of the Navajo Code Talkers went on to serve in the marines for over thirty years.

One of these heroes was Private Samuel "Jesse" Smith Sr. of the Navajo Nation. On the "day of infamy," December 7, 1941, the Japanese attacked Pearl Harbor, Hawaii. After that day, three young men attending the Albuquerque Indian School made the decision to join the marines so that they could enact revenge on the Japanese. Smith was only fifteen years old, so he had to fib to meet the age requirement; he even told his mother he had been drafted instead of volunteered. When she found out about his lie later, she told him, "No matter how old you are, I am still going to spank you." Though he entered boot camp the following year, he was not allowed to train to be a pilot, since he had not yet graduated from high school.

As per the Navajo tradition, Smith was given a blessing and shield of protection by his grandfather, who was a medicine man (*cheii*) in a sweat lodge (*táchèèh*), before his perilous journey into war. Smith's grandfather told him he was "still a punk, not a man yet," since he was so young. Smith was also given two Native artifacts to wear: an arrowhead and an eagle plume, which he never took off. When he returned, he received another blessing and returned the artifacts so that they could be sent to war with another young Navajo soldier.

Once Smith arrived at camp, he and 380 other Navajo recruits were sent immediately to Code Talker school to learn code. When Smith told the register his name, they told him he "couldn't be Sam Smith, because there were a lot of Sam Smiths." He remembered his nickname "Jesse," because it was the same name as Jesse James, and from then on, he was Sam "Jesse" Smith—as far as the United States Marines were concerned, that is. After being assigned to the Fourth Marine Division, "the Fighting Fourth," Smith was given the task of transmitting messages for General Clifton Cates and was sent to Iwo Jima to help refresh the already developed code. The beautiful Navajo language was so complicated that it was never "broken," and it was said to be far more efficient than the Morse Code system that already in use.

Through the valiant efforts of the highly top-secret Navajo Code Talkers, the United States was able to win the war. Smith fought in and survived the Battles of Rio Namur, Saipan, Tinian and Iwo Jima. He even served as a consultant for the 2002 Nicholas Cage movie *Windtalkers* before succumbing to pneumonia in 2014 at the age of eighty-nine. After his death, Private Smith was given full military and Navajo honors. There are many stories in the Navajo Nation that are just like Private Smith's, about men who fought for the United States in extremely strategic positions and saved countless American lives in the process. Private Smith said in an interview, "The Navajo Code Talkers were how the war was won…period!" We are truly indebted to these brave soldiers; they should never be forgotten.

In 1971, President Richard Nixon honored the Navajo Code Talkers with a certificate of appreciation for the patriotism, resourcefulness and courage they brought in their efforts during the war. Many Navajo Code Talkers are also Purple Heart Medal recipients.

Between 1960 and 1967, Fort Wingate was used to test the Redstone and the Pershing I missiles, and by 1971, the Department of Defense put Fort Wingate on reserve and designated it "Fort Wingate Depot Activity." Although the fort's mission ended in 1993, 6,465 acres of fort land are still used to launch target missiles at White Sands Missile Range.

Before the Long Walk, thousands of Navajos surrendered at Fort Wingate and Fort Defiance. Some would not live through the ordeal. *Courtesy of the Library of Congress.*

Fort Wingate Today

Still known today as one of the largest depositories for ammunition and ordnances in the country, Fort Wingate is not open to the public for tours. Environmental restoration at Fort Wingate is ongoing to remove the remnants of the chemicals used in ordnances from the surrounding grounds.

Directions

Fort Wingate is located twelve miles southeast of Gallup, New Mexico, on Interstate 40. To reach the fort, get off the interstate at Exit 33, and the site can be found on Highway 400 toward Gaffney, New Mexico.

The fort is visible from the road, but it is not open to the public. To access the site, prior permission must be obtained at Wingate Elementary School.

Part Two

NEW MEXICO FORTS INHABITED FOR OVER FOUR YEARS

FORT BASCOM (1863–1870)

Situated on the confluence of Romero Draw, Cow Springs Draw and Gobbler's Knob on the southside of the Canadian River, twelve miles north of modern-day Tucumcari, New Mexico, Fort Bascom was established in 1863 by Captain Peter W.L. Plumpton, of the Seventh U.S. Infantry and elements of Company F and I. The garrison was at the fort to promote settlement in San Miguel County along the Canadian River and to protect the many travelers along the Santa Fe Trail.

Brigadier General James H. Carleton, who was the acting commander of the Military Department of New Mexico, directed that the fort would be built on land leased from the owners of the old Pablo Montoya Grant. He also stated that the fort would be named after Captain George N. Bascom of the Sixteenth US Infantry, who was a casualty at the Battle of Valverde on February 27, 1862.

Although the fort was technically in New Mexico, troops from Fort Bascom were called on to help with a conflict at Adobe Walls, Texas, since the threat affected everyone in the region. Kit Carson and his First New Mexico Volunteers, who were stationed at Fort Bascom, participated in the first Battle of Adobe Walls on November 25, 1864, in the vicinity of Bent's Fort along the Canadian River in Texas. General James Carleton had turned to Carson once again to quell the advancements of the Kiowa and Comanche tribes, who were attacking the wagon trains traveling on the Santa Fe Trail. Carson and his 321 troops arrived at Fort Bascom on November 10, accompanied by 14 officers and 75 Jicarilla Apache and Ute scouts, who were commissioned from landowner Lucien Maxwell's ranch near Cimarron, New Mexico. Once at the fort, Carson's troops joined the command of Lieutenant George H. Pettis, whose artillery included two mountain howitzers in the arsenal.

Using the adobe ruins as protection, Carson attacked the 150 lodges of the Kiowas first, as they had sent out alerts to the Comanche tribes of the military's arrival. Both sides fought hard, but the soldiers were greatly outnumbered, and Kit Carson decided to retreat. Although the tribes were intimidated by the howitzers perched on the small rise, they were victorious. However, in Carleton's reports, Carson was the victor upon his return to Fort Bascom. A section of the corral wall was donated to the Canyon, Texas Museum—given in memory of Howard Hampton by Val Hampton.

Fort Bascom was incomplete, with only the adobe barracks and stone officer's quarters to form the compound. Only the foundations remain, as the fort was abandoned in December 1870. The small garrison that was left was moved to nearby Fort Union. The land was returned to the owner, John S. Watts, who had originally leased the land to the United States government. A post office existed on the site from 1874 to 1892, and Fort Bascom's name was changed to Johnson.

Located on private land, permission must be granted by the landowner before entering its location on the south shore at the horseshoe bend in the Canadian River, twelve miles north of the town of Tucumcari.

Fort Burgwin (1852–1860)

Located six to ten miles south of modern-day Rancho de Taos, New Mexico, and serving as the campus of the Southern Methodist University, Fort Burgwin was established on August 16, 1852. Although Fort Burgwin was never designated as a true fort, it was referred to as such in literature and reports. It is named for Captain John H.K. Burgwin, who was killed in 1847 during the Siege of Pueblo de Taos (or the Taos Rebellion). Burgwin is buried at the site where he died on the fort's land.

The first commander of Fort Burgwin, which was also known as Cantonment Burgwin due to the temporary nature of the site, was

Lieutenant Robert Ransom Jr., who directed the original construction starting on August 16, 1852. As with other forts, Fort Burgwin was built for defense against the Native tribes—in this case, the Jicarilla Apaches, Comanches and Utes. Travelers using the main wagon roads to the fort, which, according to Lydia Spencer Lane in her book *I Married a Soldier*, could scarcely be thought of as roads due to the ruts and boulders on them that greatly impeded travel, had to be pulled most of the way by the soldiers in wagons. At the convergence of the Rio de la Olla (Pot Creek) and the Little Rio Grande, Fort Burgwin provided the perfect respite for weary explorers who frequented the arduous journey west.

Fort Burgwin is also known for its role in the Battle of Cieneguilla (pronounced: sienna-GEE-ya) in March 1854. The battle was fought between the Jicarilla Apaches and the First Cavalry Regiment and was one of the first significant battles between the Apaches and American forces. The Battle of Cieneguilla was also reported to have been one of the "severest battles that ever took place between American Troops and the Red Indian," according to the *Santa Fe Weekly Gazette*. The battle was an unwarranted attack on the Jicarilla Apaches, who were camped near Pilar, New Mexico (known then as Cieneguilla), by the Sixty-First U.S. Army Dragoons, under the command of an overzealous First Lieutenant John Wynn Davidson, who had been ordered by Major George Alexander Blake to pursue the Indians for unknown reasons. The over 250 Apache and Ute warriors greatly outnumbered the American troops, and they were reported by Davidson to have taunted the dragoons by letting off a "war whoop" before beginning their attack.

According to conflicting survivor reports, the battle lasted for either two to four hours and resulted in the deaths of 50 Apache and 22 American soldiers, as well as 22 horses. Numerous metal points have been found at the site of the battle in the Carson National Forest, which is protected by the National Park Service American Battlefield Protection Program.

Although there were two different accounts filed on the events leading up to battle, much of the blame was placed on Davidson in both, since he could have avoided the ambush. Brigadier General John Garland took Davidson's side when he stated:

> *The troops displayed a gallantry seldom equaled in this, or any other country, and the Officer in Command, Lieut. Davidson, has given evidence of soldiership in the highest degree creditable to him. To have sustained a deadly control of three hours when he was so greatly outnumbered, and to*

have retired with the fragment of a company, crippled up, is amazing and calls for the admiration of every true soldier.

The conclusion of the military's inquiry into the battle resulted in a commendation of Davidson from Garland:

That in the battle he exhibited skill in his mode of attacking a greatly superior force of hostile Indians; and prudence, and coolness, and courage, throughout a protracted engagement; and finally, when he was obliged to retire from the field, owing to the great odds opposing him, the losses he had sustained, and the scarcity of ammunition; his exertions to bring off the wounded men merit high praise.

Cantonment Burgwin was abandoned in May 1860. A few of the remaining buildings were reconstructed in 1957 by Ralph Rounds and were used until 2004. The new buildings on the site are now known as the Fort Burgwin Research Center, which saw new construction by William Clements, chairman of the board of Southern Methodist University out of Dallas, Texas, and now serves as a satellite campus for the university. Fort Burgwin now stands as a reconstructed fort on the footprint of its original buildings in the heart of the beautiful Taos Valley. The research center for the Southern Methodist University, along with New Mexico Highway 518, is conducting a study of the ruins of Anasazi dwellings, which are reported to date back to AD 1000.

FORT FILLMORE (1851–1862)

Named in honor of President Millard Fillmore, Fort Fillmore was built by Colonel Edwin Vose Sumner, commander of the Military Department of New Mexico, in September 1851. It was the site of the only battle of the Mexican-American War fought on New Mexico soil, the Battle of Mesilla. The battle began and ended on Christmas Day 1846, when Colonel Alexander Doniphan's Missouri Regulars defeated the Mexican troops under the command of General Frias at La Salenta. The Americans received no resistance when, just three days later, they occupied El Paso, Texas.

Fort Fillmore saw the rise and fall of the Confederacy in New Mexico firsthand and was also on the route of the Butterfield Overland Mail stage, which stopped at nearby Frontera (also known as Cottonwood's Station). The cavalry soldiers of Fort Fillmore were utilized as quasi-lawmen, especially when a stagecoach or train was robbed. As with other sites, Fort Fillmore was established for the protection of travelers along the migration routes between El Paso, Texas, and Tucson, Arizona, during Western Expansion.

Falling into disrepair by 1859, the fort was spared from demolition due to the rumors of a Confederate invasion in 1861. The United States Army was able to reinforce Fort Fillmore under the command of Major Isaac Lynde. When Lieutenant Colonel John R. Baylor of the Second Texas Mounted Rifles crossed the Rio Grande into Mesilla with 250 troops on July 24, 1861, the Texans were joined by a company of Arizona Confederates and claimed Mesilla as their capital. After hearing this news, Major Lynde stormed the town the next day, resulting in what is known today as the First Battle of Mesilla. This battle resulted in a Confederate victory, after which the Union troops abandoned Fort Fillmore. The Union troops had begun marching toward Fort Stanton, when they were taken captive by Confederate soldiers east of Las Cruces, New Mexico.

Fort Fillmore was then claimed by the Confederates, and Union forces made no attempts to reoccupy the site. The fort was used by the First California Volunteers the following summer as a temporary headquarters before moving to Mesilla.

Fort Fillmore was finally abandoned by the Union in October 1862, but it continued to serve as a trading post for the surrounding farming community. The fort later fell into ruins, and the owner of the land attempted to sell, trade and even give the property to the state of New Mexico to turn the fort into a public park. Sadly, the New Mexico Parks Department had no budget money to support the ruins along with the state's other, larger sites to maintain, so it refused, which resulted in the site being leveled for the planting of a pecan orchard.

To visit the site of Fort Fillmore, which is located six miles south of Las Cruces, New Mexico, visitors should travel on US 85, one mile east of Brazito. The fort is on a pecan farm owned by Salopek Farms next to I-10.

Fort McLane (1860–1864)

First established by Major Isaac Lynde and the Seventh U.S. Infantry as Camp Wheeler in 1860 near Hurley, New Mexico, Fort McLane was also known as Fort Floyd. The fort was named on December 1, 1860, for the secretary of war under President Buchanan, John B. Floyd, who was the thirty-first governor of Virginia who resigned from the Union army to join the Confederate forces. Due to this fact, Fort Floyd was quickly renamed Fort McLane in honor of Captain George McLane.

Charged with the orders to protect the Santa Rita copper mines from Apache attacks, Fort McLane was later abandoned by federal troops on September 16, 1860, and the garrison was moved to nearby Fort Fillmore. The First California Volunteer Infantry reestablished the fort and remained there until 1864, when it was finally abandoned. This fort would also become known as Fort Webster, since it was built on that fort's original footprint and that of Fort McLean.

FORT McRAE (1863–1876)

The First California Volunteer Infantry, under the command of Captain Henry A. Greene, was the first to establish Fort McRae near Elephant Butte, New Mexico, in 1863. The fort was named in honor of Captain Alexander McRae of the Third Cavalry Regiment, who died at the Battle of Valverde on February 21, 1862. McRae served at Fort Union, Fort Stanton and Fort Craig, where he was promoted steadily and served as an escort for the governor of the New Mexico Territory, Abraham Rencher, in 1857. McRae was wounded twice before he was killed while defending an artillery battery of six guns as the commander. He was thirty-two years old at the time of his death and was buried at Fort Craig.

McRae's commander, Colonel Edward Canby wrote of McRae in his official report.

> *Among the killed is one, isolated by peculiar circumstances, whose memory deserves notice from a higher authority than mine. Pure in character, upright in conduct, devoted to his profession, and of a loyalty that was deaf to the seductions of family and friends, Captain McRae died, as he had lived, an example of the best and highest qualities that man can possess.*

McRae's body was later exhumed in 1867 in order to be taken from the New Mexico Territory and carried across the United States, from post to post, with a hero's escort. Captain McRae is now interred at the United States

Military Academy Post Cemetery in West Point, Virginia. The captain had four brothers, who fought for the Confederacy; his own father wrote to him in the hopes that he would switch sides as well—but he remained loyal to the Union army.

Fort McRae was first built to protect travelers, settlers and traders along the treacherous Jornada del Muerto (Journey of the Dead). Constant dangers including Apache attacks, a lack of water and harsh conditions prevailed along the Jornada del Muerto and plagued all who traveled this perilous route. This was a much feared, but well-traveled trail; its visitors ranged from the Spanish Conquistadors in 1598 to military soldiers in the 1800s. The establishment of a fort along this route was paramount to the settlers and community members who resided in the region. The fort also provided a great protection at Ojo del Muerto, the only water source in this area.

After the Civil War, the fort remained garrisoned by the 1st California Volunteers until August 1866. As with many of the forts in the New Mexico and Arizona Territories, Fort McRae was also garrisoned by the 38th Infantry, 125th Infantry and 9th Cavalry—the African American troops who were also referred to as the Buffalo Soldiers. Fort McRae was the only military presence within approximately thirty miles of any other installment, including Fort Craig to the north and Fort Selden to the south.

In July 1873, a great battle ensued between Captain George W. Chilson's "C" Troop of the Eighth Cavalry and the Warm Springs Apaches. With reports coming in from local ranchers of Natives stealing livestock, Chilson's men were sent in from nearby Fort Selden to pursue the raiders—the pursuit covered 465 miles. The Natives were soon trapped in a canyon, and the soldiers began to open fire. During this battle, Corporal Frank Bratling received a mortal wound to the chest, which killed him instantly. The corporal was taken to Fort McRae for burial on July 14, 1873, and he posthumously received the Congressional Medal of Honor for his participation in this battle. Bratling probably received this honor due to the forceful report that was written by Captain Chilson upon his return to Fort Selden.

Corporal Bratling's body remained interred at Fort McRae's cemetery until 1886, when President Ulysses S. Grant ordered the remains to be relocated to Fort Leavenworth, Kansas.

Fort Thorn (1853–1859)

Often described as a "miserable place to live" due to the many cases of malaria reported by the soldiers, Fort Thorn, sometimes written as Thorne, was in the upper end of the Mesilla Valley in a marshy area on the west bank of the Rio Grande near Santa Barbara and Hatch, New Mexico. The fort was named in honor of Captain Herman Thorn, a member of the Second U.S. Infantry who drowned in the Colorado River in 1849. Fort Thorn was first known as Cantonment Garland when it was established on Christmas Eve 1853 by a garrison from abandoned Fort Webster. One of the main garrisons operating at Fort Thorn was the Regiment of the Mounted Rifles—the Third Cavalry Regiment—which was established in 1846 and continues its service today.

In Assistant Surgeon P.A. Quinan's sanitary report of Fort Thorn from 1859, he gave a less than complimentary description of the fort.

> *The buildings constituting the fort are placed within a stone's throw of the swampiest portion of this flat or bottom, and in the most admirable manner, if the object be that the garrison shall inhale, for an average period of five months, the pestilential effluvia arising therefrom. The bottom referred to, presents during the hottest months, a surface of cozy mud, covered with green slime, and interspersed with pools of stagnating water, which surface is during these months gradually drying up. During the same time, a rank vegetation of weeds and grasses undergoes the process of germination, advancement to maturity, and decay. As might be expected, fevers of a malarious character, have greatly afflicted the command during this quarter.*

Built to provide protection for the settlers and miners who worked in the Santa Rita copper mines, the fort was situated between the mine and the village of Santa Barbara, which has been replaced by Hatch, New Mexico (currently the chile capital of the world). Green chiles are a staple of New Mexico cuisine, and the best are grown in Hatch. Fort Thorn was constructed with adobe brick and included a wall surrounding the fort—the only building outside the wall was the hospital. Water was provided by a 3.5-mile-long *acequia* (ditch) that funneled water from the nearby Rio Grande. The sawmill and post farms also benefited from the water provided by the often-muddy river.

Three companies manned Fort Thorn during its time of existence: the Third Infantry Regiment, the First U.S. Dragoons and the Regiment of the

Mounted Rifles. The fort was also the site of a skirmish between Union soldiers and the Confederate soldiers of the Sibley Expedition in 1861, despite the fact that Fort Thorn was officially closed in 1859. An Indian Agency was opened on the fort site and remained there until the fort was completely washed away in 1889 by a flood of the Rio Grande.

Part Three
NEW MEXICO OUTPOSTS AND CAMPS

Fort Butler (1860)

Often described as a phantom fort, Fort Butler's location was recorded on maps, and supplies and men were sent there, but it never really existed on paper. Fort Butler was the brainchild of Thomas T. Fauntleroy.

Camp Cody (1916–1919)

In Luna County, approximately two miles west of Deming, a former army encampment was garrisoned by the Thirty-Fourth Infantry Sandstorm Division. The camp was established on December 29, 1916, on a two-thousand-acre parcel of land. Originally known as Camp Deming, the training camp was eventually named in honor of the famous William F. Cody, who was historically known as "Buffalo Bill" after his death on July 20, 1917. The base's quarters housed thirty-six thousand men and sported eight hundred hospital beds.

After the Civil War and World War I, Camp Cody was used as a tuberculosis sanitorium for former soldiers. It was run by the Catholic Sisters of the Holy Cross and was transferred from the United States Public Health Service to the Deming Chamber of Commerce in 1922. The remnants of Camp Cody were ravaged and destroyed by a fire in 1936.

Camp Cody housed over thirty thousand men on a two-thousand-acre parcel of land in 1916, just before the outbreak of World War I. *Courtesy of the Library of Congress.*

CAMP OJO CALIENTE (1859–1882)

Camp Ojo Caliente (which translates to Camp Hot Spring) was never designated as an official fort, although the camp was in service for twenty-three years. With the San Mateo Mountains as its backdrop, the camp was situated on the right bank of the Alamosa River near the present-day town of Winston, New Mexico. Serving as an advanced picket post for nearby Fort Craig, the camp's main purpose was to provide protection against the marauding Navajo tribe. The government abandoned the camp after the end of the Civil War, but it was reinstated in the 1870s to serve as agency headquarters for the Ojo Caliente Reservation. Soldiers were stationed at Camp Ojo Caliente from 1877 to 1882 as support during the Indian Wars. Today, a world-class spa is located at the hot springs, and it draws thousands of weary relaxation seekers each year to its calming waters.

Fort Barclay (1851–1854)

Located two miles north of the town of Watrous, Fort Barclay was the predecessor to Fort Union and served as a forage camp. Camp Barclay was built by frontiersman Alexander Barclay, who came to the United States from England by way of Canada. Barclay was a fur trader, cattleman, corsetmaker, storekeeper, tailor, farmer and builder, who moved to New Mexico from El Pueblo, Colorado, with his wife, Teresita Sandoval.

Barclay, with the help of his associate, Joseph Doyle, built Fort Barclay on the Santa Fe Trail, which was considered a good supplier of goods and lodging. Fort Barclay was described as being a "sixty-four-foot square, with two-stories, two circular bastions and a courtyard with a well, located on the Mora River." The fort included a dam, corrals, a blacksmith shop and a supply depot within a block of adobe and log structures closed off by a heavy locking gate, but it could be described best as a trading post. It was Barclay's dream to sell his fort to the United States Army, so he was devastated when the offer was refused and the army began to build Fort Union. Although Barclay did eventually sell the fort in 1845, this initial rejection, along with the abandonment of his family and friends, is said to have contributed to his death at the age of forty-five. The remains of the fort buildings, which came to be known as Barclay's Fort, were washed away in a terrible flood in 1900.

Fort Conrad (1851–1854)

Constructed on the right bank of the Rio Grande, Fort Conrad had an excellent view of the ruins of Valverde. Originally designed to scare off the Apaches in the Rio Grande Valley who were stalking the El Paso–Santa Fe Route, the troops at the fort quickly realized that they were in a bad spot, as raids from the Navajos and Apaches increased remarkably. The commanders of Fort Conrad knew the fort had to be moved for the soldier's protection.

Under the orders of Coronel Thomas T. Fauntleroy, Brevet Major Enock Steen marched his soldiers south to set up a new fort, which was named after Colonel Louis S. Craig, who was killed during his pursuit of two deserters. Fauntleroy and Craig served together in the Second Dragoons and both hailed from Virginia. After Fort Conrad was abandoned in 1854, Fort Craig was built nine miles to the south.

Fort Dawson (1851–1852)

Fort Dawson was the brainchild of James H. Carleton, who was a protégé of General Edwin Vose Sumner and commanded the California Column. The services of the California Column were requested in the New Mexico Territory in order to counteract the Confederate invasion, which was quickly moving up from the then-Confederate Arizona Territory and Texas. Fort Dawson started out as Cantonment Dawson and eventually evolved into Fort Webster.

Fort Defiance (1851–1861)

Located in the heart of Navajo County, approximately thirty-five miles northwest of present-day Gallup, New Mexico, at the mouth of Cañon Bonito, the first Fort Defiance was soon considered a part of the Arizona Territory. The log-and-sod fort was built by troops led by Colonel Edwin V. Sumner to prevent the Navajo Nation from using valuable grazing land near the Arizona and New Mexico border. These efforts to control the tribe created strife and resentment in the Navajo people, who had lived in the region for centuries. Fort Defiance was commanded by then-colonel Edward R.S. Canby, who worked closely with Captain Henry H. Sibley to control the Navajos.

A United States soldier was once accused of tripping a horse owned by Pistol Bullet, a Navajo, during a horse race at the fort in 1856, which the Navajos saw as cheating. After the accusation, the troops backed into the fort and opened fire on the Natives while doing so; this action resulted in the deaths of thirty Navajos. Not being a forgiving people, the Navajos attacked Fort Defiance with over one thousand warriors on April 30, 1860. The Navajos, led by Manuelito and Barboncito, completely overran the garrison. Soldiers of the First U.S. Infantry under Captain O.L. Shepherd were able to turn back the Native warriors. The fort suffered one casualty and three wounded soldiers, while the Navajos suffered the loss of twenty of their men.

In 1861, Fort Defiance was abandoned and its troops were moved to Fort Fauntleroy (which would later become Fort Wingate). The fort played a role as one of the locations of surrender for members of the large Navajo Nation, who soon made the terrible Long Walk.

Fort Defiance, now in Arizona, was a part of the New Mexico Territory during the Civil War era and served as an Indian Agency. *Courtesy of the Library of Congress.*

The fort was also known as Fort Canby, and it is where, in 1863, Colonel Kit Carson set up a base of operations for his campaign against the Navajos. Fort Defiance was once again abandoned in 1864, but it reopened in 1868 as an Indian Agency for the returning Navajos. By 1870, a school was established on the site, followed by a mission church, but it wasn't until 1880 that medical services were provided for the Navajo Nation. The Indian boarding school was opened there in 1883, along with a full hospital.

Today, Fort Defiance is in Arizona and is home to the Bureau of Indian Affairs, Indian Health Service and the Navajo Nation. The Navajo Nation operates a Tséhootsooí Diné Bi'ólta', which is a Navajo language immersion school for Navajo children. The Navajo language is used exclusively in the school from kindergarten to second grade. After that, English is introduced, but it only makes up 10 percent of the curriculum. According to census records, Fort Defiance now boasts a population of approximately four thousand people. Many of the descendants of the original five hundred head of sheep given to Fort Defiance when it was first established are still roaming the reservation.

Fort Lowell (1866–1869)

Situated in some of the most beautiful scenery in New Mexico, Fort Lowell was located on the Chama River southwest of the town of Tierra Amarilla, which is close to the Colorado border. Founded in November 1866 by General John Pope, Fort Lowell was established to protect the area from the Utes. Originally called Camp Plummer in honor of Captain Augustus H. Plummer of the Thirty-Seventh U.S. Infantry, Fort Lowell was later named in honor of Brigadier General Charles R. Lowell, who died from wounds he received at Cedar Creek, Virginia. When the government was convinced that the Utes were docile, Fort Lowell was abandoned on July 27, 1869. The Indian agencies that controlled portions of the Ute and Apache tribes were transferred from Abiquiu to Fort Lowell in 1872 and consolidated in 1878, with the last rations being issued in 1881.

Fort Tularosa (1872–1874)

The last New Mexico fort in which African American soldiers were garrisoned, Fort Tularosa, was established in April 1872 by Captain Frederick W. Coleman of Company K of the Fifteenth U.S. Infantry. The fort's mission was to protect the newly opened Warm Springs Apache Reservation and agency. It was built from logs and adobe and consisted of barracks, a granary and a hospital. Fort Tularosa was later abandoned on November 26, 1874, when the Warm Springs Apache tribe (sometimes known as the Ojo Caliente Band) was moved to Ojo Caliente.

The ruins of the fort were the scene of a battle in May 1880, when Colonel Edward Hatch's Ninth Cavalry Buffalo Soldiers, commanded by Sergeant George Jordan, were dispatched to the abandoned Fort Tularosa to combat the attacks of Apache chief Victorio. Touted as the "Triumphant One," Victorio provided the troops in the western region of the New Mexico Territory with many challenges, as he practiced his guerrilla tactics to perfection.

With only twenty-five exhausted, dismounted Buffalo Soldiers from K Troop (who were also already escorting a supply train into the region) available to defend the old fort, Jordan and his men pressed on without fail to "save the women and children from a horrible fate." When the troops finally arrived at the site, they feared they were too late, but they found the fort to be secure for the moment. Jordan instructed his men to repair the stockade and prepare the old fort for the coming battle. All was quiet in the evening following their arrival until Victorio's Apache warriors seized their opportunity to attack at night.

During the confusion, all but the teamsters and two soldiers made it safely within the confines of the stockade. The Apaches decided to abandon the quest to overrun the stockade and turn their attentions to the abandoned teamsters and remaining soldiers protecting the livestock. Their moves were anticipated by Jordan, who deployed ten soldiers to reinforce the corrals—this tactic eventually drove off the attacking Apaches.

This fracas was given little notice by Colonel Hatch and was labeled a "skirmish." Even so, Sergeant George Jordan received the Congressional Medal of Honor for his leadership at the Battle of Fort Tularosa in 1890.

Since Fort Tularosa's abandonment in 1874, the only evidence that remains of its existence is its cemetery for Arizona Territory soldiers. Today, the town in which the site is located is known as Aragon in honor of a Spanish family who lives in the area.

Fort Webster (1852–1853)

Droves of people flocked to the Santa Rita, New Mexico region to participate in its rich silver and copper mining. The Mimbres Apaches and other Native tribes noticed the influx of travelers on the trails in the area and began to attack the caravans with more frequency—thus, prompting the need for Fort Webster to be constructed.

The first Fort Webster took over the remains of the Mexican Santa Rita del Cobre Fort, which had been abandoned in 1838 and given over five hundred head of sheep to sustain its troops and settlers. The members of the American Border Commission Survey Party were the first tenants of the fort in 1851, when it was known as Cantonment Dawson. The fort was soon abandoned and reoccupied in January 1852 under the name Fort Webster. This post was moved in September of 1852 from its location at the copper mine. Unfortunately, the original location, which held the remains of the fort and cantonment, were incorporated into the open pit mine of the Chino Copper Mine.

The second Fort Webster was established fourteen miles east of the Santa Rita copper mines on the west bank of the Rio Mimbres, approximately one mile from the modern-day town of San Lorenzo (which was once known as Upper Mimbres and Teel). Fort Webster was abandoned once again in December 1853, and its troops moved to Fort Thorn near present-day Hatch, New Mexico. It is reported that the second site was reoccupied in 1859 and renamed Station at the Copper Mines before it was completely abandoned in 1860.

Between the time of its establishment and abandonment, Fort Webster was briefly known by several names, including Mimbres Station, Fort Floyd (1851), Fort McLane (1852) and Cantonment Dawson.

Fort West (1863–1864)

Located at the convergence of Mangas Creek (named for famed Apache chief Mangas Coloradas) and the east side of the Gila River in Grant County, New Mexico, Fort West was a mere footnote in history. It was established on February 24, 1863, for the protection of the gold, silver and copper miners in the Gila Wilderness, and it was nestled in the Pinos Altos Mountains, away from the attacks of the local Native tribes. Captain William McCleave of the First California Cavalry established Fort West under the direction of Brigadier General James Carleton. The fort was named for Brigadier General Joseph Rodman West, who served in the First Regiment of the California Volunteer Infantry as the commander of the militia and gave the order to capture, torture and murder Apache leader Mangas Coloradas after his surrender near Hurley, New Mexico. West died in 1898 and was buried in Arlington National Cemetery. Fort West was abandoned on January 8, 1864.

BIBLIOGRAPHY

Alberts, Don E. *The Battle of Glorieta: Union Victory in the West*. College Station: Texas A&M University Press, 1998.
———. *Rebels on the Rio Grande: The Civil War Journal of A.B. Peticolas*. Albuquerque, NM: Merit Press, 1993.
Alexander, David V. *Arizona Frontier Military Place Names, 1846–1912, Revised*. Las Cruces, NM: Yucca Tree Press, 2002.
Alexander, Eveline M. *Cavalry Wife: The Diary of Eveline M. Alexander, 1866–1867*. College Station: Texas A&M University Press, 1977.
Bancroft, Hubert Howe, and Henry Lebbeus Oak. *History of Arizona and New Mexico, 1530–1888*. San Francisco, CA: History Company, 1889.
Beck, Warren A., and Ynez D. Haase. *Historical Atlas of New Mexico*. Norman: University of Oklahoma Press, 1969.
Bennett, James A. *Forts and Forays: A Dragoon in New Mexico, 1850–1856*. Albuquerque: University of New Mexico Press, 1996.
Billington, Monroe Lee. *New Mexico's Buffalo Soldiers, 1866–1900*. Niwot: University of Colorado Press, 1991.
Brayer, Garnet M., ed. *Land of Enchantment: Memoirs of Marian Russell along the Santa Fe Trail*. Dictated to Mrs. Hal Russell. Evanston, IL: Branding Iron Press, 1954. Reprint, Albuquerque: University of New Mexico Press, 1981.
Bryan, Howard. *Wildest of the Wild West: True Tales of a Frontier Town on the Santa Fe Trail*. Santa Fe, NM: Clear Light Publishers, 1988.
Bullis, Don. *The New and Completely Revised Old West Trivia Book*. Los Ranchos, NM: Rio Grande Books, 2009.

Caldwell, C.R. *Dead Right: The Lincoln County War*. Kerrville, TX: self-published, 2008.
Chacon, Rafael. *Legacy of Honor: The Life of Rafael Chacon, a Nineteenth-Century New Mexican*. Albuquerque: University of New Mexico Press, 1986.
Chilton, Lance, Katherine Chilton, Polly E. Arango, James Dudley, Nancy Neary and Patricia Stelzner. *New Mexico, A New Guide to the Colorful State*. Albuquerque: University of New Mexico Press, 1984.
Colton, Ray C. *The Civil War in the Western Territories: Arizona, Colorado, New Mexico and Utah*. Norman: University of Oklahoma Press, 1984.
Cook, James H. *Fifty Years on the Old Frontier as Cowboy, Hunter, Guide, Scout and Ranchman*. Norman: University of Oklahoma Press, 1980.
Cottrell, Steve. *Civil War in Texas and New Mexico Territory*. Gretna, LA: Pelican Publishing, 1998.
Cremony, John C. *Life among the Apaches*. Tucson: Arizona Silhouettes, 1951.
Crutchfield, James A. *It Happened in New Mexico*. Guilford, CT: Globe Pequot Press, 1995.
Delo, David M. *Peddlers and Post Traders: The Army Sutler on the Frontier*. Helena, MT: Kingfisher Books, 1998.
Foreman, Grant. *The Adventures of James Collier, First Collector of the Port of San Francisco*. Chicago: Black Cat Press, 1937.
Frazer, Robert W. *Fort and Supplies: The Role of the Army in the Economy of the Southwest, 1846–1861*. Albuquerque: University of New Mexico Press, 1983.
———. *Forts of the West, or, Military Forts and Presidios, and Posts*. Norman: University of Oklahoma Press, 1965.
Frazier, Donald S. *Blood and Treasure: Confederate Empire in the Southwest*. College Station: Texas A&M University Press, 1995.
Fulton, Maurice G. *History of the Lincoln County War: A Classic Account of Billy the Kid*. Tucson: University of Arizona Press, 1997.
Gardner, Mark L. *Santa Fe Trail: National Historic Trail*. Tucson, AZ: Western National Parks Association, 2008.
Giese, Dr. Dale F., ed. *My Life with the Army in the West: Memoirs of James E. Farmer*. Santa Fe, NM: Stagecoach Press, 1967.
Groom, Winston. *Kearny's March: The Epic Creation of the American West, 1846–1847*. New York: Alfred A. Knopf, 2011.
Haley, James L. *Apaches: A History and Culture Portrait*. Norman: University of Oklahoma Press, 1997.
Hall, Martin Hardwick. *Sibley's New Mexico Campaign*. Austin: University of Texas Press, 1960.

Bibliography

Hart, Herbert M. *Tour Guide to Old Western Forts*. Boulder, CO: Pruett Publishing Company, 1980.

Hollon, W. Eugene. *Frontier Violence Another Look*. New York: Oxford University Press, 1974.

Horn, Calvin. *New Mexico's Troubled Years: The Story of the Early Territorial Governors*. Albuquerque, NM: Horn & Wallace Publishers, 1963.

Hudnall, Ken. *Spirits of the Border: The History and Mystery of New Mexico*. Nashville, TN: Grave Distractions Publications, 2011.

Hutton, Paul Andrew. *Apache Wars: The Hunt for Geronimo, the Apache Kid, and the Captive Boy Who Started the Longest War in American History*. New York: Crown, 2016.

Jenkins, Myra Ellen, and Albert H. Schroeder. *A Brief History of New Mexico*. Albuquerque: University of New Mexico Press, 2003.

Jones, Robert C. *Ghost Towns, Forts and Pueblos of New Mexico*. Kennesaw, GA: self-published, 2014.

Julyan, Robert Hixson. *The Place Names of New Mexico*. Albuquerque: University of New Mexico Press, 1998.

Keleher, William A. *The Fabulous Frontier: Twelve New Mexico Items*. Santa Fe, NM: Rydal Press, 1945.

———. *Turmoil in New Mexico: 1846–1868*. Albuquerque: University of New Mexico Press, 1982.

Kiser, William S. *Dragoons in Apacheland: Conquest and Resistance in Southern New Mexico, 1846–1861*. Norman: University of Oklahoma Press, 2012.

Klasner, Lily. *My Girlhood among Outlaws*. Tucson: University of Arizona Press, 1972.

Lane, Lydia Spencer. *I Married a Soldier or Old Days in the Old Army*. Albuquerque, NM: Horn & Wallace Publishers, 1964.

Lavender, David. *The Trail to Santa Fe*. Boston: Houghton Mifflin Company, 1958.

Lawrence, Jennifer J. *Soup Suds Row: The Bold Lives of Army Laundresses, 1802–1876*. Glendo, WY: High Plains Press, 2016.

Leach, Nicky. *New Mexico: Off the Beaten Path, Discover Your Fun*. Guilford, CT: Globe Pequot, 2018.

LeMay, John. *Tall Tales and Half Truths of Billy the Kid*. Charleston, SC: The History Press, 2015.

———. *Tall Tales and Half Truths of Pat Garrett*. Charleston, SC: The History Press, 2016

Lowry, Thomas P. *Loma Parda: Sin City or Pastoral Paradise*. Tucson, AZ: Western National Parks Association, n.d.

McBride, James. *Interned: Internment of the SS Columbia Crew at Fort Stanton, New Mexico: 1941–1945*. Santa Fe, NM: self-published, 2003.

Metzer, Stephen. *New Mexico Handbook*. Chico, CA: Moon Publications, 1994.

Milton, Hugh M., II. *Fort Selden: Territory of New Mexico, May 1865–June 1891*. Las Cruces, NM: self-published, n.d.

New Mexico Place Names: A Geographical Dictionary. Edited by T.M. Pearce with the assistance of Ina Sizer Cassidy and Helen Pearce. Albuquerque: University of New Mexico Press, 1965.

Noble, David Grant. *Pueblos, Villages, Forts and Trails: Guide to New Mexico's Past*. Albuquerque: University of New Mexico Press, 1994.

Pittman, Dr. Walter Earl. *New Mexico and the Civil War*. Charleston, SC: The History Press, 2011.

Rickey, Don. *War in the West: The Indian Campaigns*. Fort Collins, CO: Old Army Press, 1956.

Rittenhouse, Jack D. *The Santa Fe Trail: A Historical Bibliography*. Albuquerque: University of New Mexico Press, 1971.

Roberts, Robert B. *Encyclopedia of Historical Forts: The Military, Pioneer, and Trading Posts of the United States*. New York: MacMillan, 1988.

Ryan, John P. *Fort Stanton and Its Community, 1855–1896*. Las Cruces, NM: Yucca Tree Press, 1998.

Sanchez, Lynda S. *Fort Stanton an Illustrated History: Legacy of Honor, Tradition of Healing*. Ruidoso, NM: Write Designs, 2010.

Shinkle, James D. *Fort Sumner and the Bosque Redondo Indian Reservation*. Roswell, NM: Hall-Poorbaugh Press, 1965.

Simmons, Marc. *New Mexico: An Interpretive History*. Albuquerque: University of New Mexico Press, 1977.

———. *Treasure Trails of the Southwest*. Albuquerque: University of New Mexico Press, 1994.

Simmons, Marc, ed. *On the Santa Fe Trail*. Lawrence: University of Kansas Press, 1986.

Sonnichsen, C.L. *The Mescalero Apaches*. Norman: University of Oklahoma Press, 1973.

Sparks, Dr. Twana L. *Ping Pong Balls and Donkey's Milk: A History of Tuberculosis in Fort Bayard, New Mexico*. Scotts Valley, CA: CreateSpace, 2013.

Sperry, T.J. *Fort Union: A Photo History*. Tucson, AZ: Southwest Parks and Monuments Association, 1991.

Stanley, F. (Francis). *Civil War in New Mexico*. Santa Fe, NM: Sunstone Press, 2011.

———. *Fort Craig, New Mexico*, Pantex, TX: self-published, 1963.

———. *The Fort Tularosa Story.* Pantex, TX: self-published, n.d.
———. *The Watrous, New Mexico Story.* Pantex, TX: self-published, 1962.
Taylor, John M. *Bloody Valverde: A Civil War Battle on the Rio Grande, February 21, 1862.* Albuquerque: University of New Mexico Press, 1995.
Thompson, Jerry D. *A Civil War History of the New Mexico Volunteers and Militia.* Albuquerque: University of New Mexico Press, 2015.
———. *Civil War in the Southwest: Recollections of the Sibley Brigade.* College Station: Texas A&M University Press, 2001.
Thompson, Jerry D., ed. *New Mexico Territory during the Civil War: Wallen and Evans Inspection Reports, 1862–1863.* Albuquerque: University of New Mexico Press, 2008.
Union Army Operation in the Southwest: Final Victory from the Official Records. Edited by the publishers. Albuquerque, NM: Horn & Wallace Publishers, 1961.
Varney, Philip. *New Mexico's Best Ghost Towns: A Practical Guide by Philip Varney.* Albuquerque: University of New Mexico Press, 1987.
Wadsworth, Richard. *Forgotten Fortress: Fort Millard Fillmore and Antebellum New Mexico.* Las Cruces, NM: Yucca Tree Press, 2002.
Wallen, Henry D. *New Mexico Territory during the Civil War: Wallen and Evans Inspection Reports, 1862–1863.* Albuquerque: University of New Mexico Press, 2008.
Watson, Dorothy. *The Pinos Altos Story.* Silver City, NM: Silver City Enterprise, 1960.
Weigle, Marta. *Alluring New Mexico: Engineered Enchantment 1821–2001.* Santa Fe: Museum of New Mexico Press, 2010.
Whitford, William C. *The Colorado Volunteers in the Civil War: The New Mexico Campaign in 1862.* Glorieta, NM: Rio Grande Press, 1971.
Wilson, John P. *Merchants Guns & Money: The Story of Lincoln County and Its Wars.* Santa Fe: Museum of New Mexico Press, 1987.

Articles

McMaster, Richard K. "Henry Hopkins Sibley—Confederate Commander of Fort Bliss and the Southwest." *Password: Quarterly by the El Paso County Historical Society,* Winter 1965.

Bibliography

Websites

Fort Bayard: www.fortbayard.org
Fort Craig: www.blm.gov/visit/fort-craig-historic-site
Fort Selden: www.nmhistoricsites.org/ftselden
Fort Stanton: fortstanton.org
Fort Sumner: www.nmmonuments.org and www.bosqueredondomemorial.com
Fort Union: www.nps.gov/foun
Fort Wingate: www.ftwingate.org/history

INDEX

A

Abiquiu, New Mexico 144
acequia madre 100
adobe 24, 49, 52, 53, 55, 57, 60, 66, 86, 118, 130, 136
Adobe Walls, Texas 129
Alamosa River 140
Albuquerque Indian School 126
Albuquerque, New Mexico 16, 22, 39, 44, 48, 60, 104, 108, 113, 120
Alma, New Mexico 30
Anasazi 132
Apache Canyon 110
Apaches 13, 17, 27, 28, 29, 30, 33, 34, 35, 45, 49, 50, 51, 52, 70, 75, 85, 96, 124, 131, 134, 135, 141, 144, 145, 146
Apache Wars 28, 52
Appel, Daniel M. 34
Aragon, New Mexico 145
Arapahos 116
Archaeological Conservancy 45
Arizona Confederates 133
Arizona Territory 15, 60, 86, 142, 145
Armijo, Manuel 54
Army of the West 54

B

Barboncito 123, 142
Barclay, Alexander 141
Bascom, George N. 129
Battle of Apache Pass 23
Battle of Cieneguilla 131
Battle of Fort Tularosa 145
Battle of Fredericksburg 27
Battle of Gettysburg 67
Battle of Glorieta Pass 108, 113, 114
Battle of Mesilla 133
Battle of Valverde 41, 93, 108, 121, 122, 129, 134
Bayard, George D. 27
Baylor, John R. 16, 133
Bear Springs 120, 121
Black Mesa 38, 40
Blake, George A. 131
Bonney, William H. 27, 75, 86, 87, 88, 89, 90
Bosque Farm Project 113
Bosque Redondo 75, 93, 95, 99, 100, 102, 116, 122, 123
Bosque Redondo Lake 104
Bosque Redondo Memorial 102
Bowman, Alonzo 29

Index

Boyd, David H. 35
Boyne, Thomas 29
Bratling, Frank 70, 135
Buffalo Soldier National Monument 20
Buffalo Soldiers 20, 21, 29, 31, 33, 45, 46, 49, 52, 60, 75, 116, 135, 144
Bullard, John 29
Bureau of Indian Affairs 143
Bureau of Land Management 41, 45, 53, 82
Bureau of Land Management Special Management Areas 45
Burgwin, John H.K. 130
Burro Mountains 29
Bushnell, Dr. George 34
Butterfield Overland Mail Route 22, 132

C

Cadete 95
California Column 22, 23, 27, 85, 86, 92, 122, 142
camels 68, 70
Camp Barclay. *See* Fort Barclay
Camp Cody 139
Camp Deming. *See* Camp Cody
Camp Hay 120
Camp Ojo Caliente 140
Camp Wheeler 133, 134
Canadian River 129
Cananea, Mexico 30
Canby, Edward R.S. 22, 40, 41, 42, 43, 108, 110, 113, 121, 134, 142
Cantonment Burgwin 130. *See* Fort Burgwin
Cantonment Dawson. *See* Fort Dawson
Cantonment Garland. *See* Fort Thorn
Capitan, New Mexico 74, 95
Carleton, James H. 22, 23, 27, 74, 76, 85, 92, 93, 95, 96, 100, 122, 129, 130, 142, 146
Carson, Christopher "Kit" 37, 42, 74, 75, 76, 93, 95, 99, 116, 129, 130, 143

Carson National Forest 131
Cassidy, Butch 27
Chama River 144
Chato 29, 30
Chavez, Manuel 113
Cherokee 126
Cheyenne 20, 116
Chick, Jack 30
Chilson, George W. 135
Chino Copper Mine 145
Chiricahua Apaches 28, 50
Chisum, John S. 87, 88
Chivington, John 110, 112
Choctaws 126
Cibicu Creek, Arizona 29
Cimarron, New Mexico 130
Cimarron Trail 104
Civil War 15, 16, 18, 20, 24, 27, 31, 41, 45, 46, 49, 50, 51, 52, 57, 60, 66, 78, 86, 93, 106, 114, 116, 120, 135, 139
Cochise 22, 27, 29, 50, 51, 52
Cody, William F. 139
Colfax County War 21
Colorado River 136
Comanches 13, 85, 93, 95, 116, 122, 130, 131
Confederate Arizona Territory 40, 142
Confederate army 74
Confederate invasion 16
Confederates 15, 16, 23, 38, 40, 41, 42, 43, 44, 66, 74, 86, 93, 108, 110, 112, 113, 114, 118, 120, 121, 124, 133, 134, 137
Congressional Medal of Honor 28, 70, 135, 145
Cooke, Philip St. George 49
Cooke's Canyon 51, 53, 54
Cooke's Peak 38, 51
Cooke Spring's Wellhouse 53
Cooke's Spring 49
Cooney Canyon 30
Cooney, James 30

INDEX

Cooney, Michael 30
Cooney's Tomb 30
Counter's Mesa. *See* Black Mesa
Craig, Louis S. 37, 141
Cross of the Martyrs 57, 58

D

Davidson, John W. 131, 132
Day, Mathias 29
Deming, New Mexico 36, 54, 139
Denny, John 29
Department of Arizona 71
Department of New Mexico 38
Doniphan, Alexander W. 121, 132
Doyle, Joseph 141
Dresher, Valentine 49

E

Eighth Cavalry 30, 70, 135
El Camino Real de Tierra Adentro 36, 48
Elephant Butte Lake 38
El Paso, Texas 22, 132, 133

F

Fauntleroy, Thomas T. 120, 139, 141
Fifteenth U.S. Infantry 144
Fifth Cavalry 124
Fifth Texas Mounted Rifles 42, 110
Fifth U.S. Infantry 121
Fillmore, Millard 132
First Battalion 110
First California Cavalry 60, 146
First California Infantry 22, 60
First California Volunteer Infantry 134, 146
First California Volunteers 49, 133, 135
First Cavalry Regiment 131
First Colorado Volunteers 42, 108, 110
First Dragoons 93
First New Mexico Infantry 60

First New Mexico Infantry Regiment 122
First New Mexico Volunteer Infantry 93
First New Mexico Volunteers 113, 116, 122, 129
First U.S. Dragoons 120, 136
First U.S. Infantry 142
Florida Mountains 28
Floyd, John B. 134
Fort Barclay 141
Fort Bascom 129, 130
Fort Bayard 20, 21, 24, 27, 28, 30, 32, 33, 34, 35
Fort Bayard Historical Preservation Society 35
Fort Bayard Hospital 34
Fort Bayard Memorial Cemetery 34
Fort Bayard National Cemetery 35
Fort Bayard National Historic Landmark 36
Fort Bliss, Texas 62, 71
Fort Burgwin 130, 131, 132
Fort Burgwin Research Center 132
Fort Butler 139
Fort Canby 99, 143
Fort Conrad 37, 62, 141
Fort Craig 16, 20, 37, 38, 39, 40, 41, 42, 43, 45, 46, 49, 110, 114, 134, 135, 140, 141
Fort Craig Cemetery 46
Fort Craig National Monument 48
Fort Cummings 20, 31, 32, 38, 49, 50, 51, 52, 53, 62
Fort Dawson 142, 145
Fort Defiance 96, 120, 121, 122, 142, 143
Fort Fauntleroy 121, 142
Fort Fillmore 132, 133, 134
Fort Floyd 134, 146
Fort Lowell 144
Fort Lyon 120
Fort Marcy 37, 54, 55, 57, 60
Fort McLane 133, 134, 146
Fort McLean 134

155

INDEX

Fort McRae 20, 38, 62, 134, 135
Fort Selden 20, 21, 24, 38, 60, 62, 63, 68, 69, 70, 71, 72, 124, 135
Fort Selden State Monument 60
Fort Stanton 20, 24, 33, 74, 75, 76, 78, 81, 82, 93, 133, 134
Fort Stanton Historic Site 83
Fort Stanton Naval Cemetery 81
Fort Sumner 20, 75, 85, 86, 87, 89, 90, 96, 99, 100, 102, 104, 116, 122, 123, 124
Fort Thorn 62, 136, 137, 146
Fort Tularosa 20, 144, 145
Fort Union 16, 20, 24, 32, 37, 93, 104, 106, 108, 110, 112, 114, 115, 116, 118, 130, 134, 141
Fort Union Arsenal 118
Fort Union National Monument 118, 119
Fort Union Regulars 116
Fort Webster 134, 136, 142, 145, 146
Fort West 146
Fort Wingate 18, 20, 21, 68, 99, 118, 120, 121, 122, 123, 124, 125, 126, 127, 128, 142
Fourth Marine Division 127
Fourth Regiment 82
Fourth Texas Regiment 110
Franklin, Texas 23

G

Gallo River 121
Gallup, New Mexico 120, 128, 142
Garland, John 131
Garrett, Pat 88, 90
German prisoners of war 35, 78
Geronimo 17, 27, 34, 45, 50, 52, 68, 124
Gila National Forest 28
Gila River 146
Gila Wilderness 30, 146
Glorieta Mesa 113
Glorieta Pass, New Mexico 16, 106, 110, 112

Goodnight, Charles 85
Goodnight-Loving Cattle Trail 13, 85
Grant, Ulysses S. 135
Great Western Expansion 14
Greaves, Clinton 28
Green, Tom 42, 43

H

Hatch, Edward 144, 145
Hatch, New Mexico 136, 146
heliograph 33
Hopis 124
Horseshoe Canyon, New Mexico 29
Hurley, New Mexico 133, 146

I

Indian Agency for the Apache 74
Indian scouts 52
Indian Wars 21, 45, 86, 116, 124, 140

J

Jicarilla Apaches 93, 95, 106, 130, 131
Johnson's Ranch 110
Jordan, George 144, 145
Jornada del Muerto 50, 135

K

Kearny, Stephen W. 37, 54, 57, 121
Kenney, Dita H. 34
Kiowas 20, 85, 116, 122, 129
Kozlowski's Ranch 110

L

Land of Enchantment 14
Las Animas Canyon 29
Las Cruces, New Mexico 49, 60, 72, 133
Las Vegas, New Mexico 89, 119
Leasburg, New Mexico 62, 63
Lincoln County War 76, 88
Lincoln, New Mexico 74, 76, 95
Little Rio Grande 131
Loma Parda, New Mexico 20, 115, 116

INDEX

Long Walk 75, 92, 99, 122, 123, 142
Lordsburg, New Mexico 29
Los Lunas, New Mexico 113
Loving, Oliver 85
Loving, Walter 33
Lowell, Charles R. 144
Luna County, New Mexico 49
Lynde, Isaac 133
Lyon, Nathaniel 120
Lytle, Leonidas S. 70

M

MacArthur, Arthur 68, 124
MacArthur, Douglas 68, 69, 70, 124
MacArthur, Mary 68
Mangas Coloradas 17, 45, 50, 51, 146
Mangas Creek 146
Manhattan Project 125
Manifest Destiny 14
Manuelito 123, 142
Marcy, William L. 57
Massacre Mountain 38
Maxwell Land Grant 15
Maxwell, Lucien 15, 86, 130
Maxwell, Pete 86, 90
McCleave, William 146
McComas, Charley 29, 30
McComas, David 30
McComas, Hamilton 29, 30
McComas, Juniata 29, 30
McLane, George 134
McRae, Alexander 42, 43, 134
Mesa de la Contadera. *See* Black Mesa
Mescalero Apache Reservation 76, 101
Mescalero Apaches 33, 74, 75, 76, 85, 92, 93, 95, 96, 99, 100, 101, 116, 122
Mesilla, New Mexico 15, 16, 71, 89, 133
Mexican-American War 37, 132
Mexican Civil War 125
Mimbres Apaches 145
Mimbres Station 146

Missouri Regulars 132
Mogollon 60
Mogollon Mountains 30
Mora River 141
Mormon Battalion 49
Morris, James 70
Mountain Trail 104
mules 66

N

Nana 17, 45
Navajo Code Talkers 126, 127
Navajo Nation 142, 143
Navajos 13, 50, 85, 92, 96, 99, 100, 101, 102, 116, 120, 121, 122, 123, 124, 126, 127, 141, 142, 143
New Mexico Territory 13, 14, 15, 19, 20, 21, 23, 27, 37, 38, 41, 50, 68, 86, 87, 90, 92, 93, 96, 108, 114, 115, 116, 118, 134, 142, 144
New Mexico Volunteer Infantry Regiment. 37
Ninth Cavalry 20, 21, 29, 60, 116, 135, 144

O

Ojo Caliente Band 144
Ojo Caliente Reservation 140
Ojo del Gallo 120
Oñate, Don Juan de 36, 65
125th Infantry 20, 31, 60, 135
Organ Mountains 62

P

Pablo Montoya Grant 129
Palace of the Governors 54, 57
Pecos River 95, 100, 102
Pershing, John J. 33, 124
Picacho Peak 62
Pigeon's Ranch 110

Index

Pilar, New Mexico 131
Pinos Altos Mining District 27
Pinos Altos Mountains 146
Pistol Bullet 142
Plummer, Augustus H. 144
Plumpton, Peter W.L. 129
Pope, John 144
Preservation 24
Pueblo Revolt 58
Purple Heart Medal 127
Pyramid City, New Mexico 30
Pyron, Charles L. 41, 110

Q

Quaker Guns 40, 41

R

Radium Springs, New Mexico 60, 62, 74
Raguet, Henry 42, 43
Rancho de Taos, New Mexico 130
Red Horse Vineyard Bed and Breakfast 44
Regiment of the Mounted Rifles 136, 137
Revolutionary War 17, 41
Rio Bonito 74
Rio de la Olla 131
Rio Grande 21, 22, 36, 38, 39, 41, 46, 60, 63, 113, 133, 136, 137, 141
Rio Grande Valley 141
Rio Mimbres 145
Roberts, Benjamin 41
Robledo Camp 66
Robledo, Don Pedro 65
Robledo Mountains 60
Roosevelt, Theodore 22
Rough Riders 22
Ruidoso, New Mexico 95

S

Sacramento Mountains 76

San Antonio–San Diego Mail and Passenger Services 49
San Carlos Reservation 45, 52
Sandoval, Teresita 141
San Lorenzo, New Mexico 146
San Marcial, New Mexico 48
San Mateo Mountains 140
Santa Clara, New Mexico 36
Santa Fe National Cemetery 46
Santa Fe, New Mexico 22, 39, 40, 44, 49, 54, 57, 60, 65, 108, 113, 115
Santa Fe Plaza 54
Santa Fe Railway 118
Santa Fe Trail 13, 104, 110, 115, 130, 141
Santa Rita del Cobre Fort 145
Santa Rita Mountains 27
Santa Rita, New Mexico 145
Schropshire, John S. 110
Scurry, William 41, 43, 110, 112, 113
Seboyeta, New Mexico 120
Second Dragoons 141
Second Regiment California Volunteer Cavalry 22
Second Texas Mounted Rifles 41, 133
Second U.S. Infantry 136
Selden, Henry R. 60
Seventh Texas Mounted Rifles 42
Seventh Texas Mounted Volunteers 110
Seventh U.S. Infantry 129, 133
Shakespeare, New Mexico 30
Sheerin, John 70
Sherman, William T. 45
Sibley Expedition 137
Sibley, Henry H. 16, 22, 39, 40, 41, 42, 43, 44, 108, 110, 113, 142
Sibley's Brigade 22, 23
Siege of Pueblo de Taos. *See* Taos Rebellion
Silver City, New Mexico 27, 29, 36, 54
Sixteenth US Infantry 129
Sixth Cavalry 33
Skeleton Canyon 52
Slough, John P. 110, 113

Index

Smith, Samuel "Jesse" 126, 127
Snowy River Cave National Conservation Area 82
Socorro Garrison 37
Socorro, New Mexico 36, 37, 48
Sombre Robledo Mountain 65
Spaniards 13
Spanish-American War 22
Spencer, Lydia 131
Stanton, Henry 74
Station at the Copper Mines 146
Sumner, Edwin V. 54, 85, 93, 132, 142

T

Taos, New Mexico 93
Taos Rebellion 130
Tenth Cavalry 20, 21
Texas Mounted Rifles 41
Third Cavalry Regiment 134, 136
Third Infantry Regiment 136
Third U.S. Artillery 22
Third U.S. Cavalry 35
Thirteenth U.S. Infantry 124
Thirty-Eighth Infantry 31, 49, 135
Thirty-Fourth Infantry Sandstorm Division 139
Thirty-Seventh U.S. Infantry 144
Thompson's Canyon 29
Thorn, Herman 136
Tierra Amarilla, New Mexico 144
Treaty of 1868 101, 102
Treaty of Guadalupe Hidalgo 15
Tres Castillos, Mexico 45
Tséhootsooí Diné Bi'ólta' 143
tuberculosis 34, 35, 76, 77, 81, 139
Tucumcari, New Mexico 129
Turkey Mountains 106
Twenty-Fifth Infantry 21
Twenty-Fourth Infantry 21
Twenty-Fourth Infantry Band 33

U

Union 38, 39, 40, 41, 42, 43, 74, 93, 108, 110, 112, 113, 121, 133, 134, 135, 137
United States Army Signal Corps 33
Utes 93, 130, 131, 144

V

Valverde Land and Irrigation Company 45
Valverde, New Mexico 38, 141
Veterans Administration 34
Victorio 17, 20, 27, 30, 45, 50, 52, 124, 144, 145
Villa, Pancho 27, 125

W

War Department 20
Warm Springs Apache Reservation 144
Warm Springs Apaches 28, 30, 135
Watrous, New Mexico 119, 141
West, Joseph R. 146
White Mountains 95
White Sands Missile Range 125, 127
Williams, Cathay 31, 32, 33
Wingate, Benjamin 121
Winston, New Mexico 140
World War I 34, 125, 126, 139
World War II 35, 78, 125, 126

Y

Yuma, Arizona 22

ABOUT THE AUTHOR

Donna Blake Birchell is a native of the Land of Enchantment. Although Donna has traveled to and lived in many different states, her heart always brings her back to New Mexico. Her career as a library cataloguer gave her a great love of books, which she surrounds herself with at every chance. As a child, her father, William Blake, instilled in her a love of history as he performed a lengthy travelogue during their weekend travels throughout New Mexico and Texas.

Writing is a passion that began early for Donna, and she wrote her first short story at age twelve. As the author of eight books featuring New Mexico and Texas, it is a dream for her to bring the fascinating history of her beloved region to as many readers as possible so that they may marvel at the sheer magnitude of the stories still untold. Recently, photography has gripped her soul by giving her another much-needed creative outlet that complements her books perfectly.

The thrills of finding additional information through research, hearing a fresh take on an old story and playing detective to unearth new clues about the rich history of the area are what keep Donna on this fantastic journey.

Donna's proudest accomplishments are her two sons, who live in northern New Mexico and east Texas, which is much too far, in her opinion, from her Carlsbad home.

www.ingramcontent.com/pod-product-compliance
Lightning Source LLC
Chambersburg PA
CBHW040251170426
43191CB00018B/2373